A WITCH LIKE ME

The Spiritual Journeys of Today's Pagan Practitioners

By

SIRONA KNIGHT

NEW PAGE BOOKS
A division of The Career Press, Inc.
Franklin Lakes, NJ

A Witch Like Me

Edited by Jodi Brandon
Typeset by Eileen Dow Munson
Cover design by Lu Rossman/Digi Dog Design
Printed in the U.S.A. by Book-mart Press

To order this title, please call toll-free 1-800-CAREER-1 (NJ and Canada: 201-848-0310) to order using VISA or MasterCard, or for further information on books from Career Press.

The Career Press, Inc., 3 Tice Road, PO Box 687,
Franklin Lakes, NJ 07417
www.careerpress.com
www.newpagebooks.com

Library of Congress Cataloging-in-Publication Data

Knight, Sirona, 1955-
    A witch like me : the spiritual journeys of today's pagan practitioners / by Sirona   Knight.
      p. cm.
    Includes bibliographical references and index.
    ISBN 1-56414-539-5 (pbk.)
      1. Witches—United States—Bibliography. 2. Witchcraft. I Title.
    BF1408 .K55 2001
    299—dc21

                                                2001044268

To my dear friend and innovative
editor, Mike Lewis,
who suggested the idea for this book
the day we first met.

And to
President John F. Kennedy,
who will always remain an inspiration
and guiding light in my life.

ACKNOWLEDGMENTS

L oving thanks to my husband Michael and my son Sky for their love, courage, and optimism. Heartfelt and grateful thanks to my family and friends, especially my father, mother, stepfather, and stepmother for being open-minded, encouraging my writing, and for always loving me, regardless of what I do or say.

Many thanks and heartfelt appreciation to Lisa Hagan at Paraview, who is my dear friend and agent. And I would like to especially thank and acknowledge the thirteen prominent practicing witches who made this book possible: Dorothy Morrison, Trish Telesco, A. J. Drew, Phyllis Currot, Raven Grimassi, Silver RavenWolf, Raymond Buckland, Lady Sabrina, Timothy Roderick, Gerina Dunwich, Skye Alexander, Marion Weinstein, and Z. Budapest. May Goddess and God bless you all, now and forevermore!

I would also like to gratefully thank and acknowledge everyone at New Page Books, especially my publisher Ron Fry for having the courage and insight to print books such as this one. Continued thanks to my extraordinary editor and friend, Stacey Farkas, for her fine editing work and for being such a compassionate and understanding woman. You shine brightly, Lady! Blessings and thanks to my most excellent publicist, Laurie Kelly, for her friendship, enthusiasm, and kindness. And many thanks to Michael Langevin, editor and publisher of *Magical Blend* magazine, for his continued support and friendship.

The Road Not Taken
by Robert Frost

Two roads diverged in a yellow wood,
And sorry I could not travel both
And be one traveler, long I stood
And looked down one as far as I could
To where it bent in the undergrowth;

Then took the other, as just as fair,
And having perhaps the better claim,
Because it was grassy and wanted wear;
Though as for that the passing there
Had worn them really about the same,

And both that morning equally lay
In leaves no step had trodden black.
Oh, I kept the first for another day!
Yet knowing how way leads on to way,
I doubted if I should ever come back.

I shall be telling this with a sigh
Somewhere ages and ages hence:
Two roads diverged in a wood, and I—
I took the one less traveled by,
And that has made all the difference.

CONTENTS

Introduction: Standing up for What We Believe   11

Chapter 1:   My Story   21

Chapter 2:   Dorothy Morrison   51

Chapter 3:   Patricia "Trish" Telesco   61

Chapter 4:   A. J. Drew   69

Chapter 5:   Phyllis Currot   79

Chapter 6:   Raven Grimassi   97

Chapter 7:   Silver RavenWolf   107

Chapter 8:   Raymond Buckland   117

Chapter 9:   Lady Sabrina   125

Chapter 10:   Timothy Roderick   135

Chapter 11:   Gerina Dunwich   147

Chapter 12:   Skye Alexander   159

Chapter 13:   Marion Weinstein   167

Chapter 14:   Z. Budapest   177

Afterword   185

Appendix: Internet and Books Listings   191

Index   201

About the Author   207

STANDING UP FOR
WHAT WE BELIEVE

I n 1987, I traveled to Virginia in order to be closer to my Craft teacher. While we were staying in Virginia, my husband Michael and I wanted to publish a crystal newsletter. After typesetting it, we called a local printer, who said to bring it right by. The next day, I received a solemn call from the printer, who said he could not print the newsletter because of its content. It was only a basic pamphlet with information on crystal healing. There was nothing about Witchcraft or the Goddess in it, but still the printer refused to print it because of its perceived religious content. So much for freedom of speech.

This incident made me sit down and rethink my child-hood images of what America, democracy, and freedom were all about. I realized there were vast discrepancies between the ideal and the real. I felt alienated from the masses, and I went searching for a spiritual path that made sense to me, a spirituality that explained life and my purpose in it better than the standard Christian concepts of good and evil.

I was attracted to the concept of spirituality not being exclusively male-oriented, of it being an integration of the female and the male. To think that the Divine was only male, even when I was a young girl, seemed absurd. After all, men don't give birth; it is in the womb of the mother where all life originates. The combination of the Goddess and God produces Oneness, a concept that includes the infinite whole of everything that is, was, and will ever be. From the One comes the Whole, and from the Whole comes Oneness.

Where Books Come From

The idea for this book arose when I was invited by Ron Fry, the publisher of New Page Books and Career Press, Inc., to attend BEA (Book Expo America) in Spring 2000. During the first day of the trade show, I did tarot readings and promoted my books at New Page's booth, and afterwards, I went with the New Page group to a sumptuous dinner. Over the course of the meal, editor Mike Lewis said he thought it would be interesting to do a book about the personal experiences of some of the more prominent Witches in the United States. He wondered if I would be interested in creating a book about my personal story as a Witch, along with editing the stories of other Witches. I had been kicking around a similar idea for a book and already had the title for him. I immediately replied, "Great idea! We'll call it *A Witch Like Me*."

The American Ideal

A short time after BEA, my son Skylor and I were at our local library. After browsing around in the kids' section, he brought over a juvenile version of *Profiles in Courage*, written by John F. Kennedy. I picked up the book and started thumbing through it. I had read the book many years before, and when I started scanning the pages, I remembered President Kennedy's ideas—that you had to have the courage to stand up for what you believed, even if that wasn't the popular thing to do.

Suddenly a voice in my head said, "That's right—just like Wiccans have to stand up for their beliefs today." I felt an immediate connection that seemed to send me through a portal to another dimension, and my hair stood on end. I realized that what Kennedy was writing about in his book is still happening in the modern Wiccan Movement today. In both cases, people are still very much standing up for what they believe in, politically and spiritually.

In 1955 (the same year as my birth), John F. Kennedy, recovering from a back injury, wrote *Profiles in Courage,* which chronicles the lives of United States senators, including Daniel Webster and John Quincy Adams (who later became president). He wrote about men who stood up for their political and personal beliefs, even when those beliefs could have cost them their livelihoods and social standing.

The Basis of Our Freedom

A Witch Like Me follows in this same tradition. This book is also about individuals—in this case, Wiccan authors who have had the courage to stand up for their spiritual and personal beliefs by writing their books. These beliefs and practices come under the heading of Wicca and reflect a new religion that is interwoven throughout the roots of humankind.

America was founded on the basis of religious freedom. The people who originally migrated from Europe did so for religious and economic reasons. From the Quakers to the

Puritans, they all came to the "New World" in order to escape religious persecution. This religious freedom is the reason why modern Wiccans thrive in this country.

Unfortunately, this freedom sometimes gets trampled on. Witches sometimes experience prejudice towards their Wiccan ways by the mainstream religions. Part of what this book chronicles is this prejudice and how the Wicca Movement of the 21st century is moving, at light speed, beyond these traditional stereotypes and prejudices.

The Dynamic Growth of Wicca

Wicca is the fastest growing spirituality in America—some say in the world! Rather than being a step behind, Wicca makes an effort to bring the past into the future and, in the process, creates a spirituality that is Earth- and Nature-oriented and forward-thinking, a path that recognizes the Divine Feminine and Masculine in everything.

In order to survive as a species, humanity needs to become aware of the needs of the Earth, our principal source of life. By disconnecting with the Earth, we are disconnecting with ourselves. So not only are we destroying our physical environment, but we are also disrupting our spiritual connection to ourselves. We become aliens on our own planet—strangers in a strange world. Today, so many people are fearful of going out into Nature. We have become afraid of who we really are: a divine part of Nature.

The Divine Truth

Divinity is not an exclusive male club. There isn't some merciless, larger-than-life male deity sitting on an opulent throne (as many patriarchal religions would have us believe). Instead, the Divine is bipolar. It is both male and female. The female, because she is the source of creation, is without a doubt part of the Divine. How she ever became regulated to the rib of a man is beyond me. It must have taken some fancy footwork and an amazing public relations campaign to get people to believe that one!

The simple truth is the female procreates and the male fornicates. It takes both, but the actual creation is from the female, not the male. From the interaction of the male and female, life arises and is born into this reality from the mother. From this perspective, divinity is male *and* female, never one or the other. Any spirituality that preaches one or the other does not embrace the whole of divinity. (Needless to say, cloning really throws a wrench into all of this!)

In essence, Wicca is a modern phenomenon that derives from traditional spiritualities, such as the Celtic, Egyptian, Roman, and gypsy. From these traditions comes the practice of Folk Magick, which uses the cures and practices that originate from the melting pot of cultures that make up this country. This is why the United States has become the meeting place for so many diverse ideas that make up modern spirituality.

We Shall Overcome

Wiccans are also more tolerant of other religions than they are of us. For example, a few months ago, my mother was talking with a middle-aged Christian woman who lives in Kentucky. When the subject of Witches came up, the woman said if she ever met a Witch, she would kill the person. So much for religious tolerance. Thank Goddess, it was a Christian who said that, not a Wiccan!

Even though people make idle threats, they still translate into religious intolerance, an intolerance that has infiltrated this country during the past several decades. Witches have become discriminated against much in the same way that Blacks, Asians, Latinos, or any other minority group have.

Religious tolerance was at the heart of the founding of this country. From Puritans to Quakers to Catholics, everyone came to this country under the umbrella of religious freedom as outlined in the Constitution of the United States. This is what makes us different from both Fascism, on the Right, and Communism, on the Left. America is a nation that is home to all, regardless of creed, color, or religious persuasion.

14 Witches

At the heart of this book are the stories of 14 Witches who seek to follow a different path and drummer, each bringing our light and music into the world through our writing. Each of us shares our personal experiences growing up, often knowing we were different at an early age, usually by having a psychic or magickal ability. The personal stories in this book are the stories of people who have chosen to embark on a new and often controversial religious path: the Wiccan path—much in the same way our Founding Fathers established this country. As we begin a new millennium, we are the ones who will help to lead us into a new era of humanity, one popularized by love, compassion, and a reverence for others, ourselves, and this planet. The Goddess and the God are reflected in all of us. It is up to each of us to realize this.

I selected these particular authors for several reasons. I have met almost all of them in person. I have known Trish Telesco, Dorothy Morrison, A. J. Drew, Skye Alexander, Raven Grimassi, Silver RavenWolf, Gerina Dunwich, and Marion Weinstein for quite a while, and I consider them my friends and colleagues. We have talked in person, met at public events, eaten meals together, and, now and again, helped each other get book contracts. A. J., Trish, Dorothy, and I have all been doing the Real Witches Ball together for several years now. A.J. hosts and organizes it, and we are the honored guests. Some of us gab for hours on the phone (thank Goddess for five-cents-a-minute long distance). We continuously correspond through e-mail, do Internet chats together, and conduct interviews together for radio and magazines. Trish and I have written books together, and we even appeared together on *The Richard Bey Show*—and survived to tell about it! (She made love potions and I turned someone's nasty boyfriend into a toad!)

Those authors who I haven't met are all well-known Wiccan authors whose books I have read and enjoyed and whose work I admire. I hope to meet each one of them in the near future.

20 Questions

I asked each of the authors the same 20 questions and answered them myself in Chapter 1, which is my story. Some authors responded to all the questions. Others responded to most of them. Still, others focussed on their area of interest or on particular stories that had the greatest impact on their lives. This is why you will find a connecting thread and a continuity between the personal stories.

The 20 questions I asked each of the authors are:

1. When exactly did you know you were a Witch? Did you always know you were a Witch? Did you know when you were a child?

2. How did you come to walk down the Wiccan path? What were some of the reasons you embraced the spiritual philosophy of Wicca?

3. What form of Wicca do you practice?

4. What is your relationship with Deity like? Do you have favorite Goddesses and Gods that you call upon in your spiritual practice?

5. Do you practice magick every day? Every month? In what ways?

6. What was your first magickal experience?

7. Please describe your first ritual magick experience.

8. What do you feel are the most empowering aspects of Wicca?

9. What were some of your life-changing experiences as a Witch?

10. How has Wicca transformed your life? What was your life like before being a Witch, and what is it like now that you are a Witch?

11. Have you experienced any healing benefits from Wicca? Is so, please describe them. Also, do you perform healing works if you are in a group or coven?

12. If you have children, has being a Witch influenced the way you educate them? Are your children following the Wiccan path? Do you practice Wicca as a family?

13. Does your family (other than your nuclear family) know you are a practicing Witch and Wiccan author?

14. Does your family accept your spiritual practice and profession?

15. Do you consider your group or coven your extended family? How so, and how does this belonging help empower you and the other members of your group?

16. Has being a Witch changed the way you are accepted in your community? Have you ever been discriminated against because you are a Witch?

17. What is your opinion of some of our modern fictional Witches, such as Harry Potter, Gandalf, Buffy, Samantha Stephens, and Sabrina? Do you think they are accurate or beneficial stereotypes? Why or why not?

18. How do you feel about Witchcraft going mainstream? What do you feel the reasons are that more and more people of all ages and backgrounds are embracing Wicca?

19. Do you feel you are "a mover and a shaker" in the Wicca Movement, and, if so, what is your expectation of Wicca in the future?

20. Have you done an Internet chat or workshop on Wicca? Do you frequent the Internet? How has it affected your spiritual journey?

The True Test of Courage

After reading this book, it is my hope that you will realize that you are not alone in your experiences. After many years of suppression, the Goddess is emerging as an equal spiritual entity to the God. This is not meant to supplant the male energy, but rather to enhance it. Deity is both male and female. We are one. We are at a crucial point in human history: Our institutions and perceptions of the world are rapidly changing. The Goddess and the Wicca Movement have contributed to that change in a positive way. We carry the light into a new millennium, and it is up to us to accept responsibility for our intentions and their results. What we do with the new millennium is up to us. We are the ones who cultivate this Earthly garden, the garden that will feed the future generations. If we plant, water, and cultivate this garden with love and compassion, then this is what we will reap as our harvest.

This is a book about the faith and courage of ordinary people. It's also about the fact that a person's need to maintain self-respect is more important than his or her need to be popular with others. As Wiccans, our integrity, faith, hope, and practices are stronger than our need for public approval. Keeping your faith is a true test of courage, and each of us must decide the course we will follow. These profiles of Wiccan authors are stories of courage. My hope is that they will offer you hope and provide inspiration. But please remember: They are not meant to *replace* courage. For this you must look into your own mirrored face.

1

MY STORY

My first magickal experience was Shamanic. I was 7 years old, sitting on a three-legged, wooden milking stool in a neighbor's cattle barn. In front of me, a dead deer hung on a meat hook, its life force flowing out of it. Blood dripped from its mouth and nose. I vividly remember that its eyes were open, and they seemed to stare unwaveringly at me. I was left alone in the barn for a few minutes when my parents and the neighbor rancher (who had killed the deer) went to the local grocery store. I stared at the deer and felt horrible that someone I knew had been cruel enough to shoot and kill such a beautiful creature.

I began praying for the soul of the deer and crying at the same time. Through my tears, I saw the eyes of the deer come alive. The spirit voice of the deer told me very clearly that she wasn't really dead at all, that her body was just dead, that she couldn't feel her body any longer, and that she wasn't in any pain. I stopped crying, and it was like the scene in the movie

Starman where the deer comes back to life. The spirit of the deer stepped out of the dead body in the form of a bright, white, luminous image of a deer-woman. She invited me to go with her to where deer go when they die: a magickal place filled with sunlight, clear streams, brilliant blue lakes, and hills of unending green grass.

It was a place where nothing ever died, where there was always plenty of food, and where there was no struggle, fear, pain, or death. I thought it was the most beautiful place I had ever seen in my life. A few minutes seemed like a day as I walked with the deer-woman through this Otherworld, a place that felt very real to me.

When my parents returned from the grocery store, I told them that the deer wasn't really dead at all. I told them about the deer-woman spirit and the beautiful place she had taken me to. I was so excited, I couldn't stop talking. They smiled and told me to settle down and that it was just my imagination. They assured me that the deer was indeed dead, but I knew what I had experienced. It was just too vivid not to be real!

I Knew I Was Different

From that moment on, I felt like I couldn't rely on what my parents said, because they just didn't seem to be having the same experience I was. They didn't see the lights around things or hear any of the voices I did. It seemed as though they were sleeping and refused to wake up, no matter what I said or did. They seemed alien to me, and I must have seemed pretty alien to them. Needless to say, I spent a lot of my time outdoors with the dogs and cats.

Another magickal experience that altered my view of reality came one day at the age of 9 when I was riding Poncho Via, one of the quarter horses on my father's cattle ranch.

Crossing a ravine that took us up a small hill, I met up with a friend from school who was riding a female horse that was in heat. After about 10 minutes my friend rode off toward home, and Poncho took off at a full canter after her. I found myself on the back of a horse that was moving a lot faster than I had ever ridden before.

My legs dangled along his side, kicking him, which moved him even faster. I was frightened and screaming, which didn't help. Straight ahead, and not that far ahead, I saw the edge of a deep granite quarry filled with water. I thought I was going to die. I was terrified. I tried to pull the horse up hard by the reins, but he wouldn't slow down. In a moment that seemed to go by in slow motion, I felt a tap on the shoulder and a loud masculine voice told me that everything was going to be all right.

I saw a small tree just up ahead in that same instant and I reined Poncho hard to the right around the tree. In a flash, the horse made 90-degree turn and then came to a dead stop. I scrambled off Poncho as fast as I could and walked him all the way home.

Later, I found out that Poncho was trained as a cutting horse, used to round up and separate cattle in a corral and tight spaces, so he was most likely doing what he was trained to do when he turned so suddenly around that tree. But even now, I recall that voice, and I am positive there was a divine hand at work—the hand that doesn't always give you what you want, but more often than not, does give you what you need.

A Reflection of My Culture

As is the case with many of the authors in this book, I did not envision myself as a Witch when I was younger, at least not in the traditional sense. I grew up watching television shows such as *Bewitched, Gilligan's Island, The Monkees, Star Trek,* and *Twilight Zone*, as well as *I Dream of Jeannie, Ozzie and Harriet, Leave It To Beaver, The Donna Reed Show,* and *Father Knows Best.* So you can safely say I don't exactly fit the "wicked Witch" stereotype. I'm pretty much a reflection of my culture and, as a result, a lot closer to the Samantha Stephens–type of Witch. There have been many occasions when people have come up to me at author events and said, "You look too normal to be a Witch."

I must admit, I enjoyed the Samantha Stephens character in *Bewitched* and always cheered for Glenda the Good Witch in *The Wizard of Oz.* I was drawn to movies such as *Bell, Book, and Candle,* and even named my black cat Pyewackat, but I never really stopped to consider that I might be a Witch. I had dreams of being a writer, not a Witch.

The Gifts from My Parents

My parents are native Californians, as are my husband, son, and myself. We are lucky to live in the Golden State, because we blend right in with the many alternative religions and lifestyles that California is famous for. I was born in San Jose, California, and as a child, I remember the house being filled with lots of books.

I was raised in an intellectual environment with plenty of liberal ideas, and I cut my teeth at cocktail parties for the academic elite.

Both of my parents were college professors. My father taught anthropology and history, and my mother taught linguistics and English. When I was a child, my parents hosted get-togethers and parties where they and their colleagues discussed some of the more progressive ideas of the 1960s while listening to Bob Dylan, Pete Seeger, Joan Baez, and Peter, Paul and Mary records. I always listened in until I was sent off to bed.

This lifestyle contrasted completely from my summer vacations, which were spent in a small alpine mountain valley in northern California where we didn't have a television. For entertainment, we listened to Wolfman Jack on a portable transistor radio at night. I rode horses and chased after cows on my family's cattle ranch all summer. A friend once asked me which world, the academic one or cattle ranching, had the most BS in it. I'd have to say it was a toss-up!

Being first-generation Italian, my father focused on the importance of education and learning how to do things for oneself. He read Italian fairy tales to me or, more often than not, made up fantastic stories before I went to sleep at night. When I think of my father, I always imagine him sitting at his desk writing poetry. He always had folklore, history, and anthropology books around the house, and he often encouraged me to open and look through them.

When I was 14, my father got me a summer job at the college where he taught. My job was to transcribe *The Ways of Mankind* series of recordings, which were about indigenous cultures and their spiritual practices. I learned a lot about Shamanic practices and journeying. I was so fascinated by the information that I started reading as much as I could find on tribal cultures, Shamanism, and folklore. This was about the same time that my mother gave me a paperback copy of Carlos Castaneda's book, *The Teachings of Don Juan.* It was also when I started going to Berkeley to buy copies of *The Berkeley Barb* newspaper and to San Francisco to listen to the street musicians at the Cannery and Fisherman's Wharf.

My deep love for music is interwoven into my spirituality and work. Listening to music often helps me to hear the Divine, to tap into Oneness. I almost always listen to music when I write. For me, music provides an "altered" state of divine consciousness, where I can directly link up with Deity and the Elemental powers.

When you consider my father's love of music, a love that he shared with me, it's not surprising that music has the effect it has on me. We always listened to country music when we drove around in my father's truck. There was Johnny Cash, Jimmy Reeves, Loretta Lynn, and Hank Williams. My father also liked to lie back on the couch and turn the volume way up on classical records such as Vivaldi, Mozart, and Sibelius. He did the same thing with Madame Butterfly and Frank Sinatra records. (I still listen to Old Blue Eyes, but not to Madame Butterfly.)

Although my love for music and folklore, my poetic abilities, and my independent streak stem from my father, my creative abilities come more from my mother. She has always encouraged my creativity. She taught me how to make things, sew, embroider, cook, and garden. As I child, I remember my mother playing the piano and singing, gardening, making me a dress for a school dance, and reading books.

She always corrected my English and encouraged me to read and to write my own stories, even as a young girl. She would often tell me that she wanted the next book she read to be one that I wrote.

The Gifts from My Nana

When I was growing up, neither of my parents was religious. We didn't go to church as a family. In contrast, my Italian nana was a devout Catholic. She was the person who introduced me to the Mother Mary and all the Catholic saints. She was also the one who showed me how to say a prayer when I was lighting a candle. To me, a spirit of prayer always dances on the flame.

Nana was the person to whom I turned for help and support much of my adult life. It's common knowledge in the

Pagan community that Catholics make the best Wiccans. From my experience, I'd have to agree. I think it's probably because of a shared respect and love for rituals and also because divine communion and rapport are spiritual concepts that are a mainstay for Wiccans, much as they are for Catholics. This was so in my life.

I stayed with Nana on the weekends when I was young. She would braid my long hair, pin it on top of my head, put a fancy white scarf over my head, and take me to church on Sunday morning. That was when the entire service was conducted in Latin. It was much more dramatic and fun, because I didn't understand a word the priest said. I listened to the cadence of his voice, and the sound would push me energetically out of my body. I would suddenly find myself looking down at Nana and the entire church congregation from what seemed to be the ceiling, high above the pews. It was an interesting way to spend Sunday morning—and a lot more fun than just sitting there. This was long before I even knew what an out-of-body experience was. Needless to say, Nana spent a great deal of her time tapping me on the hand to get my attention when it was time to kneel.

Where Do Witches Meet?

I figured out early on that it was unwise to discuss the magickal experiences I was having with my family, so I began looking for other people with whom I could share my ideas and experiences. One person I met early in my adventures was my spiritual partner and husband, Michael. We met in high school when I was 13 and he was 17. He was pointed out to me by a divine hand—literally!

Walking to class on a cloudy and windy October day, I saw him. Then I saw a giant hand come out of the clouds and point to him. I heard the words in my head, "He's the one."

Giant hands coming out of the clouds and pointing at strangers wasn't something I had experienced before (or have ever since), so I paid very close attention. Being 13, I automatically questioned the experience and wondered if it was real. I wondered silently to myself, *Who is this guy, and what was that hand thing?*

I have known Michael for more than 31 years now. He, as well as our son, practices Wicca. We are still strongly connected after all these years. Michael is the only person that I know who accepts me for who I am. No matter how strange or crazy my question or idea is, he listens and gives me suggestions without blinking twice.

But then, Michael is a little out there, too, which reminds me of the line from a Marshall Crenshaw song, "If you weren't a little bit out there too, I just wouldn't bother with you." I would say that most Wiccans *are* a little bit out there, pushing the envelope and boundaries of society. That's what Wicca is all about: a spiritual revolution!

Even as a young girl, I always pushed the envelope and was considered a rebel. My love for independent, sometimes revolutionary, thinking comes mostly from my father. He has always been a forward-thinker and was blackballed by Senator McCarthy in the 1950s for speaking out against him. Because of his experiences, he has always encouraged me to stand up for what I feel is right. I've never been one for going along with the program just because everyone else was doing it.

I recall the time when I sang in a high school talent show. We were allowed to choose our material, and my friends and I decided to do the Vietnam protest song, "Ohio." The teachers in charge tried to talk us out of it, but we insisted. We got up on stage and started singing, and right when we got to the part of the song that goes, "What if you knew her and found her dead on the ground?" the principal unplugged the public address system. We were using microphones and electric guitars, so that pretty much put us out of commission. Instead of giving up, we started singing a little louder, and after about a minute the entire student body stood up and started singing with us. The principal was livid. His face turned red and he was grimacing at us in the stage wings.

We repeated the song a couple of times with everyone singing together. The teachers had their mouths open; they looked stunned and a little frightened. I always thought this was twisted, because it was the high school seniors who faced being drafted into the military and going to Vietnam after graduation, not the teachers.

Summer Vacation Studies

During summer vacation when I was 15, I took a trip to British Columbia, Canada, where I first learned about the mysteries of the tarot. One of the camp counselors had brought his acoustic guitar and a Rider-Waite Tarot deck. When he wasn't playing music or driving the bus, he read everyone's cards. When it came time to read my cards, he told me to pick a card from the deck to signify myself. I chose the High Priestess card, but I never knew why until many years later.

From the moment I saw and touched the tarot cards, it was as if I had come home. I felt a profound connection to the cards and the metaphysical energies they represented. It was more an experience of remembering—not learning—how to use the cards. This immediate and lasting connection with the tarot eventually led to the creation of my own tarot deck (The Shapeshifter Tarot), which was a divine gift from the Celtic god Lugh on Lughnassad.

During summer vacation when I was 16, my mother took me to England and Scotland to visit our family manor, which is about 30 miles from Coventina's Well in Northumberland.

She felt it was important to get in touch with our family roots. What I discovered on this quest, other than a few skeletons in the closet, was a roughly bound, inches-thick volume of family history. The book lists, among other things, my Celtic ancestors, who date back to Edward II, and are described as a clan numerous and of considerable antiquity up on the border between England and Scotland.

One of my ancestors, Sir Bartram Reveley, lies interred in the chancel at Mitford Church. His epitaph reads, "Here lyeth a generous and virteous knight. He was descended from a race of worshipful antiquities, loved. Rest Bartram in this house of clay, Reveley unto the later day." In my family tree, I also discovered a few more knights, a cavalier, a governor, a couple of infamous authors, and even James Smithson, who was a British chemist, a mineralogist, and the founder of the Smithsonian Institute.

As we traveled by car through England, Wales, and Scotland, it was as if by being there, walking on the land, seeing the graves of my ancestors, touching the trees and stones, and talking with the people, something triggered inside of me, something that had been hidden away but was waiting to be reborn. Walking in Hyde Park in London, browsing the attic of an antique clothing shop in York, sitting atop the windswept hills of my family home in Northumberland, and watching the tide come in on Lindesfarne Island—all of these things permanently transformed me. Everything seemed so familiar. This was particularly true of Edinborough Castle. When I walked through the ancient gates of the castle, it was as if I had walked through a portal to an Otherworld. Time stood still for a few moments and that familiar chill flooded my body. The hair on the back of my neck stood straight up. It was as though I had walked through a gateway to another time and place, yet it was as real as walking out my back door.

The Impossible Is Actually Quite Probable

This Otherworld experience spurred me to actively seek out more information when I returned home from my trip abroad. I did a research paper on the Druids in high school that year. That was when my mother offered to take me to the college library for reference books. Once I discovered all of the books at the college library, it seemed my thirst for knowledge about the Druids, folklore, Shamanism, miracles, and metaphysics would never be satiated—and so far it hasn't been.

In college I was accepted into a progressive cluster school program at Sonoma State University called The Hutchins School of Liberal Studies. In this program, students work with their faculty advisors to come up with a personal curriculum based on each student's needs and desires. Classes are structured as discussion groups, where faculty and students discuss subjects such as comparative religion and the writings of Socrates and Plato in a seminar style.

While at Hutchins, I put together a device that took Kirlian photographs. I used the device to conduct experiments on people's auras. I was particularly interested in how feelings of love expanded someone's aura. For me, Kirlian photography was wonderful because it validated and exposed the energetic light fields around people that I had been seeing since I was a child. I had learned early on never to say anything to anyone else about them. Somehow I felt I had finally been let out of the closet. During much of my childhood, I could never say what I really saw, heard, or felt. Kirlian photography represented one of those minor victories, where I finally felt that not only was I sane, but I was on a path that led me into the future of humanity. Today Kirlian photography is used in hospitals for diagnosing illnesses such as cancer.

My fascination with Kirlian photography and parapsychology led to the creation of my own set of Rhine telepathy cards. I remember sitting alone at the kitchen table and working with the deck of Rhine cards that I had made. As a divine dare, I remember wondering out loud if anyone had ever correctly guessed all of the cards at one sitting. The statistical odds for doing so are way off the charts. I shuffled the cards without looking at them and then stacked them in one pile, face down, on the table surface. On a sheet of paper, I wrote down the order I thought the cards were in. I turned over the Rhine cards, one by one, and they were in the exact order I had written on the paper. I couldn't believe it, but I checked the order several times. I poured myself a cup of tea and just sat there for the longest time. From then on, I have always felt that doing the impossible is very possible—quite probable, in fact.

Learning the Power of Crystals

After receiving my bachelor's degree in liberal arts, I pursued a graduate degree in consciousness at John F. Kennedy University, where I was able to meet and converse with New Age luminaries such as Charles Tart, Henry Dakin, Jeffrey Mishlove, Thelma Moss, and Stanley Krippner. I later went on to receive my master's degree from California State University, Sacramento.

Working in the San Francisco Bay Area was very exciting for me, as these men were the leading experts in parapsychology, with Stanley Krippner and Thelma Moss being pioneers in Kirlian photography and aura studies. At the time, the Bay Area was the center of the New Age Movement, but I still felt a spiritual longing and hunger that needed to be satisfied.

While I was driving home from work one day, I tuned into a radio talk show. Eminent scientist Marcel Vogel was describing his work with healing crystals. As he talked I felt something begin to resonate within myself until tears welled up in my eyes. I didn't know why I was feeling so emotional, but I went with this profound feeling and called Marcel, beginning a divine connection and wonderfully supportive friendship that lasted until his death in 1991.

Marcel was a devout Catholic who went to Mass every morning at 8:00 a.m. He admitted that he had some problems with Catholicism—for example, when he tried to teach a group of students Zen meditation.

Marcel was a believer in the strength of right thought and the power of prayer. He was also one of the most incredible crystal healers I have ever had the fortune to meet and work with.

One of my most vivid memories of Marcel is the time when a heart patient came into his laboratory asking for help. As the man walked into the lab with his wife, you could see he wasn't well. His skin was pale white, almost blue, and he couldn't walk without assistance. He could barely raise his arms. Even when he raised them a tiny bit, you could see in his face that the movement caused him great pain.

After introductions were made all around, Marcel grabbed his four-sided healing crystal and began a crystal healing on this man. After working on him for about 45 minutes, not only could the man raise his arms over his head, but he was able to do so without any pain. His cheeks filled with color, and he walked out of the lab without any assistance and got into his car. It was the most amazing demonstration of crystal healing that I have ever had the honor to witness.

Two weeks later the man was back in Marcel's lab saying that he had been to his doctor, who professed amazement over the man's rapid recovery.

Meet Max, the Crystal Skull

In the 1980s, Marcel Vogel, holder of hundreds of U.S. patents on luminescent paints, phosphors, and liquid crystals, was at the forefront of crystal research. I often went to his lab in San Jose, where we talked, exchanged ideas, and did experiments. He also collected old texts on alchemy that he had me read through and catalog. He often used me as a guinea pig in his experiments.

With Marcel, if you showed up in the middle of an experiment, you became part of the experiment. On one occasion, Marcel blessed me with the opportunity to work with one of the crystal skulls, which have been reported to be of both ancient and alien origins. As soon as I walked into the lab, he handed me the skull, and said, "I would like you to meet Max."

I introduced myself to Max and sat with him in my lap for most of the day—that is, when we weren't shining different frequencies and hues of colored light through his eyeballs and mouth. As I touched the skull here and there, I could sense that it was akin to a huge computer filled with information. I just didn't know exactly how to boot it up. I felt very different after spending the day with Max, and since then, I have had a particular interest in the sacred, and most likely alien, power of the crystal skulls.

Thought Equals Energy

As I do, Marcel saw the greater significance in everything. He always asked me what I thought the implications were in the work we were doing. He felt that everything was interconnected. He would often repeat the concept that "thought equals energy." With enough thought energy, Marcel believed, anyone could manifest things into reality. Thought resembled a carrier wave. He demonstrated to me in several experiments that energy does indeed respond to what we think, feel, say, and do.

On one visit to his lab, I had the opportunity to work with the De La Warr Radionics Camera, which was a thought-photography camera. We thought the image of a star, and when we looked at the photographic plate, the image of a star appeared. We thought of a circle and the image of a circle was there on the plate. This, as many of my experiences at Marcel's lab did, permanently changed the way I view reality.

From particles and waves to thought fields, everything is energy, from the simple to the complex and back again. Energy, and the fact that it can be influenced, acts as the basis of magick. For me, the Divine is an energy that is inherent in all things, animate or inanimate, which is why I call it Oneness. At a certain point, everything is energy, which is the point where everything comes together as One.

My Initiation into Druidism

I was introduced to the Druid tradition by a friend. We were discussing metaphysics, and he told me that he was a part of a secret Druid tradition that had specific magickal teachings.

He explained the concept of Oneness and the basics of an ancient Welsh mystery tradition called the Gwyddonic Druid tradition that had been brought to America in the late 1700s.

Gwyddonic Druidism is an evolution of Pagan concepts and practices. It is a spiritual practice without the dogma that bogs down most religions. For me, this was one of its charms. I liked the open-ended concepts and practices, so I decided to be initiated. I collected my ritual tools as quickly as I could, made my wand, and within a month, at 9:45 p.m. on Hellith's Day, during the full Blood Moon, I was initiated.

Everything came together on the night of my initiation, but not without a few hitches. Earlier in the evening, I didn't know if I was going make it to my own initiation when the drive train of the car I was riding in busted right off. I was with a friend, and here we were in the middle of the not-so-wholesome part of Sacramento, and I was wondering if I was doing the right thing. We began walking to a nearby house where a little girl was playing outside. She was very friendly and told me that her name was Tara. I asked her if I could use the phone. I called the place where the initiation ritual was going to take place and someone came to pick us up.

When we arrived, I was introduced by the same friend who had provided the introduction to the group. The person at the door welcomed me with a hug and the words, "Merry Meet, Merry Part," and then handed me a green ceramic chalice of wine called the greeting cup. Next, the High Priestess took me into a darkened back room, put a black cloth blindfold over my eyes, and tied my wrists together with a string. After this she handed me the death cup and told me to drink it. It tasted awful. She told me it represented the death of my old self—and that tonight I was being reborn. After a while, I was led out to the living room, still blindfolded, where I could hear a lot of people milling around me.

The initiation began, and I was taken into the four directions, from gate to gate, led and prompted by my Hound, the person in the Druid tradition who leads an initiate around during the initiation. I was told the passwords, "Perfect Love and Perfect Peace." Then I was told to get down on my hands and knees. I was guided, crawling, through the open legs of the High Priestess. When I got up, my blindfold was taken off and the ties on my wrists were cut.

Next, the High Priest told me to take hold of the crossed athame and wand and to draw in as much divine power as I could and to connect with the Goddess and God as intensely as I could. I remember merging with my surroundings and then grasping the tools and merging with them as well. My body heated up to the point of being uncomfortable. Millions of pinpoints of blue-white light filled the room; it felt as though there was a lot of divine company with us.

Once I let go of the ritual tools, everyone in the group greeted me with a hug and the passwords, "Perfect Love and Perfect Peace." Everyone looked as if they were glowing with light, some brighter than others. Then everybody took turns kneeling at my feet. I felt like the Goddess being worshipped. When they were all done, I piped up, "Can we do that again?"

Next, the group formed a circle and I was led to the center. They chanted, "Triana, Triana, Triana!" nine times, bringing the divine energy of the threefold Goddess into the circle. Triana is my sponsor Goddess. (I chose her because about a week before my initiation I had a dream about a regal, confident, and beautiful goddess. She showed me her three faces: one young, one middle-aged, and one very old. Then she gave me a mirror and showed me my three faces. She told me her name was Triana.) We did the blessing cup ritual, the Hellith's Day ritual, and full moon healings. We all did a spiral dance around the room at the end of the rituals, jumping up and down to build the energy and shouting the names of the goddess Kerridwen and the god Kernunnos. After catching our breath, we shared a great feast together with lots of conversation about magick and plenty of music and song.

Going Public

One of my overwhelming desires when I started writing my first book, *Greenfire: Making Love with the Goddess,* was to publish information that was given to me bit by bit when I was initiated by people who seemed to want to use the teachings to control the process and me. I felt that the teachings of the Gwyddonic Druid tradition needed to be made available to all who felt an affinity for them. After *Greenfire* was published, a small group who wished to keep the information secret chastised me for publishing the secret teachings, but the many people who seek a path to Oneness congratulated me for finally making the information public.

This is also why I finally published *Exploring Celtic Druidism*, which describes, step-by-step, my initiation, training, and the rituals of the Great Days of Gwyddonic Druidism as they were presented to me by my teacher.

I think that this secretiveness and controlling attitude of the "old guard" are two of the main problems with Wicca. Because of past persecutions, the teachings have always been secret and unavailable to the public. Because of the secrecy, the mainstream population, unfortunately, views Witches and Wicca in a stereotypical fashion. These misconceptions are slowly changing as more Wiccan authors write about their experiences and share the teachings they were taught.

I now work with a wonderful Druid group in northern California. The College of the Sun is an extended family. We have been initiating more and more new members, and interest seemingly continues to grow. Most of the people who come to be initiated are women and men who want to learn how to connect more deeply with the Divine and create positive change in their lives. They truly want to come alive and begin anew.

We Are Everyday People

One of the most powerful things about Wicca is that it's a new religion. I'm always amazed that I am alive at a time when a new religion has come to the forefront. One of the best things about Wicca is that it's perfectly acceptable to be an eclectic Wiccan. You can gather ideas and concepts and then put them together into a spiritual practice that works for you. It's a personal path—not dogmatic, but very creative. It's also open-ended and represents a living spiritual path that is always changing, moving, and evolving. There is no savior who has been dead for two thousand years, no hierarchy of power when you connect with the Divine or with the light. I don't think there has been such a powerful movement since rock 'n' roll!

The Wiccan movement is a reaffirmation of the very ideals that brought our ancestors to America, to the "New World." This country was founded by people having the courage to stand up for their spiritual beliefs. We are born, we live and die, civilizations come and go, but ideas live on through generations. Wiccan ideas, such as healing the Earth, Oneness, compassion, and truth, are re-created by each succeeding generation as it comes of age.

As to the question, "Who are Witches?" I reiterate the reply given by Sly and the Family Stone: "We are everyday people." Most everyone is looking for a savior, someone to lead them out of their personal hell, but it is only through our connection with the Divine that we reach something beyond the mundane. Wicca is a divine revolution, a revolution from within and without. Wiccan practices are a methodology for encountering and merging with the Divine and making magick on a personal level that has divine implications. Our connection to the Divine is what is essential. Disconnection from the Divine causes illness, anger, and suffering, as well as pain, grief, and a lack of compassion.

Many religions teach their adherents to be fearful of the Divine. The Divine Energy, no matter what name you call it, is not waiting to cast you out with your first indiscretion.

People make mistakes; this is part of the learning process. Spirituality, which is basically the process of connecting energetically to the Divine, should reward you for your progress, not penalize you for your mistakes. One of the great things about Wicca is that it empowers people and teaches self-responsibility. The Wiccan Rede says, "An ye harm none, do what ye will." In this responsibility is the divine power to realize your dreams and achieve your goals.

Knowing firsthand that creation comes from the female or feminine aspect of life, I have always found it hard to believe that the Divine is inherently male. Divinity is about creation, and creation is about the Goddess, not the God. It is in the womb of the Goddess that we were all created, and each of us continually thanks our mother for the fact that we are even here in this life.

From the womb of Oneness we are birthed into this physical reality, and through our experiences, we can either move forward or backward. The choice is ours. The promises of Paganism are love, earth, sexuality, the coming together of energies, Oneness, and everything that we were born with and born to be. Wicca is about working with Spirit and connecting with the light in Nature and in all living things, with everything. All things, whether animate or inanimate, are imprinted with Spirit. Everything is Oneness and a union of all polarities.

Honoring the Female

Wicca is one of the first spiritual traditions to recognize and revere the female as well as the male. Wicca is the first modern spirituality to see the Divine as the combination of both male and female energies. As a girl, I was never allowed to sit at the head of the table at family gatherings; men always held that seat of honor. I resented that seating arrangement, because it was the women who cooked the meals and did all of the work. I longed for a spirituality that gave women something more than a space in the kitchen. Although I like to cook and eat, I did not think my life began and ended in the traditional female roles.

The time of religions that cater to men has passed. Women now have the right to equal status. This is the way of the future. Men need to accept women as part of the Divine, not as subservient. The intelligent men I know already do this. After all, it is the female who gives birth in Nature. Instead of downgrading the man's role, which is obviously still vital and essential, Wicca gives women and men equal status as integral and complementary parts of the Divine. This is why Wicca is so appealing to me.

Wicca is the first modern spirituality to accept women as equals. We were not made from Adam's rib and we don't walk two steps behind the man the way a dog does. Don't misunderstand me: I love men, especially thinking, creative men. I have been in a relationship for more than 31 years with a very sensitive and loving man. However, I believe that women and men are equal in energetic and divine terms. There are certainly differences between our physical bodies, but divinely, we are the same. We are one. Without the feminine, life ceases to exist. It is the union, not the struggle, of the female and male that produces life. The war between the sexes is part of an outdated mythology, not part of the new age that is dawning. Face it: Women and men can't survive without one another. There is a built-in union.

In many ways women and men seem the same, and in other ways, as Dr. John Gray puts it, they act as though they are from different planets—Venus and Mars, according to Dr. Gray. That is because feminine and masculine energies are polar opposites, in the same way hot and cold are. The merging of these polarities into one is what Divinity is all about, particularly in terms of Wicca. In Oneness, you do not lose your individuality. Instead, you reaffirm your individuality and its connection to the whole. From this connection comes the real power of magick.

I felt the power of this magick when I wanted to have a child. This desire was along the lines of a miracle, as we had been trying unsuccessfully for 11 years, and in the meantime one of my ovaries had been surgically removed because of endometriosis. I was told by one doctor with no bedside manner that my chances of getting pregnant were a million to one. Undaunted, my husband and I started doing healing works on my remaining ovary. My husband did hands-on healing and together we brought in the Divine as much as possible. This was also when we began using sex magick, with the goal being to conceive a child. I also began taking Weleda homeopathic remedies.

Wicca Is a Family Tradition

In 1991, interestingly on the same great day as my initiation, Hellith's Day, during the full moon, our son Skylor was born. He has been a guiding light in my life since then as well as a constant inspiration in ritual. From the beginning, he took to ritual like a fish to water. He was initiated into the Druid tradition when he was 7 years old.

I think it's essential that our children be included in ritual. From its earliest roots, Wicca has always been a family celebration. Too many of the rituals I have attended keep the children in another room watching television. I think this is a huge mistake! Children need to be seen and heard in family ritual and magick. It becomes crucial that we teach our children well, as they are the ones who will carry the magick into the future.

Connecting with the Divine

To make magick, you first need to connect with the Divine. Many people don't understand that if you don't make that primary connection, there is no magick. Children naturally know this. You can mouth the words, play with your sword, wave a wand, and burn all the candles you want, but you still won't create magick unless you merge with the Divine, symbolized by the Goddess and God, mother and father of all manifested reality.

For me, the universe has consciousness—it's living. That is why I think that it's essential to go outdoors in Nature and commune with the Divine. It's much easier for me to get a channel through to the Sacred when I'm outside with my feet on the earth and surrounded by the Elements. When I step outside under the trees, I can feel the Goddess and God right there next to me, everywhere around me.

The spirit of the Divine resides in the sacred land, and I've often felt that Deity is merely a different tense of being. For me, each goddess and god has her or his distinct voice. They have distinct qualities that make them individual and exactly who they are. My favorite goddesses and gods, the ones I work with on a daily basis, are Celtic, such as Kerridwen, Kernunnos, Anu, Math, Gwydion, Lugh, Rosemerta, Rhiannon, Triana, Angus, Boann, and Dagda.

When I work with deities, I like to know who I'm working with. I have found that certain deities work best in certain areas of life. For example, the Celtic god Lugh is the perfect sponsor god when you are doing business. The Celtic goddess Coventina can be a helpful sponsor goddess when you are trying to conceive a child.

From personal experience, I have also found that rapport with deities from other pantheons is welcome, and from time to time, depending upon my intention, I work with Buddha, Shiva, and Shakti, as well as Kali, Krishna, Isis, and Bast. I have also had an interest in Odin and other Norse goddesses and gods, such as Freya, Frey, Thor, and Heimdall, together with the three fates of Urd, Skuld, and Verdandi, since high school. My school's football team was the Vikings, and we sang our school song to Odin, the strongest one!

Divine blessings and voices remind me of the miracle of life, of being alive and in the flesh. The Divine to me encompasses all of the spirits and souls of those who have been born, have lived, and who have died. All of us breathe the same air. All of us love and experience joyful times as well as feel sadness and pain. We are one.

The Divine Power of Mother Earth

Unfortunately today, so many people never even go outside, much less pray or practice Wicca outside. At least five days a week, people go from their houses to their cars and then to work. At the end of the day, they get back into their cars and go to the store, back home, or to the gym. Then they do it all over again the next day. A lot of people don't even go out into their backyards anymore or keep a family garden. Some even put concrete or gravel over the grass in their yards, claiming that it's just easier. Making magick indoors or online is fascinating and productive, but it's not the same as stepping outside under the trees, sun, moon, and stars and communing with the Divine, with the sacred power of the Earth and Elements.

When you get in touch with the divine power of the Earth, you start taking better care of the land. Most Witches have great compassion toward the Earth, animals, and plants, and they respect the Earth Mother. We realize the value of the

Earth. There are still people who throw trash out their car windows or dump trash all over the land instead of hauling it to the dump. These are people who desperately need to get in touch with the divine energy of the Goddess. They really need to get a more divine life!

This reverence for the Earth, who is the mother of all, is at the heart of Wicca. We realize the need to treat our Mother as sacred rather than trashing, mining, logging, and polluting her.

Again, the Sacred Union

Besides helping me to realize my divine connection with the Earth, Wicca has also helped me get in touch with the feminine energy. As I noted before, feminine and masculine are polarities of energy. For the last few thousand years, the masculine polarity has been overly stressed. This has manifested itself in more aggressive behavior that resulted in wars and international confrontation, as well as a more business-like, scientific way of doing things, resulting in a detached view of the world. Wicca is bringing a change to this worldview, whereby the feminine polarity comes into florescence—and not at the expense of the masculine polarity, but rather in conjunction with it. This, again, is the sacred union. Because of this union, there is less fear and meanness from Wiccans, a trend that I hope continues far into the future.

Love and compassion are the foundations of all religions, so if Wiccans have love and compassion for one another, then I feel we are moving in the right direction. Divided and struggling with each another, we can accomplish very little. Working together as one, we can forge a united and brilliant future for Wicca and the Earth, the vision of which now only resides in our imaginations. This is a promising aspect of Wicca, as are such movements as Patriotic Paganism, where Wiccans vote and support basic American values such as family traditions. I know many Witches who use the American flag in ritual. After all, Witchcraft is very American—early American.

We Are not "Hollywood Witches"

To the great displeasure of the Religious Right, I don't feel that Wicca is just a T-shirt or tattoo fashion statement. It's an official and legal religion, as well as a spiritual and sacred path. Unfortunately, the Hollywood Witch media-hype just fuels the misinformation about Witches, and this gets really stale. Many other practicing Witches that I know agree. Practicing magick is a lot spicier and much more fulfilling than the tasteless pablum Hollywood is spoon-feeding us. The most imaginative thing Hollywood directors could do is to hire reputable Witches as consultants for their movies. Then the magick would really begin! (I hope they are intelligent enough to do that with the *Harry Potter* movie.)

Personally, I adore the whole Harry Potter hoopla, as does my family. It's creating a whole new generation of Witches. Wicca is really coming of age in a big way and J.K. Rowling's *Harry Potter* books are helping the movement. A lot of children, teenagers, and adults are reading the books, and pretty soon, they will all want to know how to translate fiction into fact and make real magick themselves. Mainstream is embracing Wicca, and Wicca is definitely going mainstream. The obvious pitfall to this enormous boon for Wicca will be commercialism. Making more dollars and cents unfortunately seems to be the primary focus of publishers, film-makers, and others in the business, so there is very little sense being used. I think that's why there is a bevy of spellbooks being published right now and a lack of books on valid Wiccan practices.

There is divine rapport, intention, and visualization involved in magick. Unfortunately, some practitioners don't even go there. They just think, *I'm going to do this just the way it's written in this book and it's going to work.* That's pure insanity! I explain again and again to people that you have to make the ritual or spell your own. And more importantly, in order to make magick, you must merge with the Elements and with divine energy. You must focus your attention and energy toward your magickal goal.

Get out of the Cyber-Broom Closet!

I think that diversity is one of the primary strengths of Wicca. This is reflected in the Internet, for example. The great thing about the Internet for Pagans is that it has brought us out of isolation, out of the cyber-broom closet and online in large numbers. Pagans from all over the world now get together and chat, do rituals, and exchange information and spells.

As with most new technology, the Internet fascinates me. Its potential as a tool for weaving Witches together is phenomenal. It brings Wiccans together that normally would ever be able to come together, from all over the world. When you do a cyber-ritual, you can participate with Wiccans across America and in Canada, Mexico, Australia, Cambodia, Belgium— virtually anywhere!

I use the Internet to keep in touch with fellow Wiccan authors, with group members, and with business associates. I receive e-mail from Witches all over the world, do international chats (such as the International Pagan Conference), and respond to questions. I recently published a book with Trish Telesco called *The Wiccan Web,* which stemmed from a conversation we had a few years ago about being Web Witches. Now we are working together on another Wicca Internet book called *The Cyber Spellbook.* I have to admit I'm amazed when I go into a search engine such as Yahoo, search for "Sirona Knight," and see hundreds of listings.

Looking Ahead

I still question everything, just as I did at 13, and I often wonder where all of this will lead us. I love writing books, and as a contributing editor for *Magical Blend* magazine for the past several years, I have had the remarkable opportunity to talk with authors, including those in this book, and musicians such as Ravi Shankar, Donovan, Brandon Boyd, Crispian Mills, Barrett Martin, Ottmar Liebert, and Chi Chong. It's been an incredibly empowering experience, because I now know what seems impossible is actually very possible. If someone told me when I was listening to Donovan records as a teenager that my husband, son, and I would be having tea with him and his lovely wife Linda in San Francisco when I was 40, I would have never believed it. Now I realize the impossible happens all of the time. It's magickal!

Having the opportunity to talk with and meet such interesting authors and musicians has directly influenced my view of reality and has encouraged me to further push the envelope. When I talk with interesting people, meet a lot of creative people, and rub elbows with people who have diverse (and sometimes radical) ideas, it's delightful, not to mention that it stimulates more ideas and discoveries. I can't imagine myself being satisfied with a 9-to-5 job anymore.

Looking ahead, I still hope to be writing books in 20 years. Writing has become my lifeline, my way to connect the dots. I can't help but wonder what my work and the work of the other Witches in this book will have created. Will our work have made a significant difference? Will we have created more congruence, connection, world peace, kindness, and love? My hope is that our work will help more people wake up, come alive, and shine with compassion and love toward one another, animals, trees, plants, and the land.

An eminent psychologist said that my book *Dream Magic* was dangerous because it showed people how to control their dreams and that it had the potential to topple nations and institutions. I certainly hope so! Things could use some toppling and changing. There is so much sadness, hunger, poverty, ignorance, and pain in the world. I know in my heart that we, as Wiccans, can make a positive difference at home and in our communities.

It's time that we take responsibility for our dreams. The concepts of making magick and asking for what you want have finally come of age. It is time to dream the dreams you choose and dare to dream and to directly participate in your sleeping as well as your waking life. These concepts may seem radical to the corporate-herd mentality, but they are music to my ears and the ears of many others.

As a young girl, some of my earliest recollections are of seeing and hearing President John F. Kennedy on television. In the early 1960s, he represented a generation of Americans filled with hope and high expectations. As our first Catholic president, President Kennedy ushered in a time of religious tolerance; there was a feeling that everyone should be allowed to pursue their dreams. Everything was possible, and magick was definitely in the air.

I realize that the patterns of history run in a circular motion, and I think these times of magick and of hope and pursuing dreams are once again presenting themselves as they did during the Kennedy years. People throughout the land are proclaiming themselves Wiccans without regard to public pressures, including social and economical ostracism. Once again, people are showing the courage to stand up for their heartfelt beliefs.

Face it: The times are changing, and change they will. We all know that things are not as they seem. Things do indeed go bump in the night, most every night. There are people who have regular ET contact experiences—normal folks, maybe your sister or brother—or maybe even you. We know the world is changing, and it's changing at light-speed! And no matter how much you go into denial, it's not going to go away.

Wicca is the one spirituality with the tolerance and open-ended qualities to integrate these light-speed changes. Wicca is tolerant of just about everything as long as it doesn't harm or hurt others. That's one of its best—and revolutionary—qualities. Oneness includes just about everybody, everything, and more!

For a Witch like me, Wicca is a spiritual path filled with the bright promise of the future of humankind. It is a path of union and Oneness that may well protect us from ourselves and save the Earth from its present course of destruction. I will forever be hopeful and optimistic. Everything is possible as long as magick is in the air. So mote it be!

DOROTHY MORRISON

T he most important thing that I would like people to
understand from my writing is that magick all stems
from your own creativity and imagination. Creativity
is the biggest part of that. There have been several authors in
the past who have suggested that things be done this way, this
way, and only this way. They suggest that if you don't do it
their way, it won't work. I think you can do magick any way
you want, as long as it works for you. The gods have a sense of
humor. If you want it bad enough, you can't screw it up. People
need to realize this. Magick is here to make your life easier,
not more difficult.

For Dorothy Morrison, award-winning author of
Everyday Magic, In Praise of the Crone, The Whimsical
Tarot, *and* Enchantments of the Heart, *magick was a
part of her life even before she was born.*

For most folks, their date of birth is the single most important event in their lives. I am not most folks. My real life began on a hot August day, some eight months and three weeks before I was born. In fact, if it wasn't for my father's trademark stubbornness, I might not have been born at all. The doctors at the Scott and White Clinic insisted that my mama have a radical hysterectomy. Not tomorrow, not next week, but immediately—right then and there. Daddy told the doctors, "We are getting a second opinion." He then yanked Mama out of the clinic quicker than you could say, "Blessed Be," put her in the car, and together they drove away. It was a good thing he did, because Mama was already pregnant with me!

Reflecting on her almost non-beginnings, it's not surprising that Dorothy chose to walk the magickal path.

After all, I was a magickal child, but it wasn't until 20-odd years ago that I had the slightest idea what the magickal path was or where to find it. Even then, I wasn't sure who to trust or how to take the next step. The Lady always seems to provide for Her children, even if they don't know they belong to the fold, so before long, the folks who could help me crossed my path.

Stubbornness Runs in the Family

A Witch with a particularly colorful heritage, Dorothy stems from a long line of folks who changed the world with their own special touch.

I'm the product of German and Scottish royalty, Confederate colonels, Texas rangers, and Swamp Fox patriots. I'm descended from Edgar Cayce, a state poet laureate and the man who instituted the Texas library system. I also had a great-great-aunt who poisoned an entire regiment of soldiers to save the wounded Confederates being nursed back to health in her attic. A smattering of ministers, lawyers, doctors, and government agents fill in the blanks. Even though some of their tactics were a bit unconventional, they all knew what they wanted, knew how to get it, and, through pure stubbornness, kept at it until they succeeded.

Keeping her origins in mind, it's no surprise that Dorothy was a stubborn child.

I refused to speak until I could say complete sentences. I refused training wheels for my bicycle because those were for babies. I felt that brown was ugly, so I refused to wear it. Much to Mama's dismay, I refused to do a lot of things that other people, including my parents, thought I should do.

Rebellion Started Early

When she was 5 years old, Dorothy simply refused to continue praying to Jesus.

Devout Catholics, my parents were absolutely horrified about my decision. Even after raising three other girls, they couldn't cope with this situation. They begged me, pleaded with me, and threatened and punished me, but none of it did any good. Finally, Mama summoned all her wits and asked for an explanation. The answer was simple: I told her that praying to Jesus was a complete waste of time. It meant I'd have to wait around and see if he would approve of my wishes. On the other hand, there was no holdup when praying to Mary. She was his mother, and I figured that even Jesus Christ himself wouldn't have the gall to disobey Mama! My mother breathed a sigh of relief and made me promise never to speak of it again. I was, after all, going to Catholic school the next year.

And Never Let Up!

Catholic school brought Dorothy even more aggravation—
and not just for her, but also for the nuns who taught her.

I'm not sure that Sister Carol ever recovered from my first year at school. She simply could not understand why I kept coloring outside the lines, and in colors other than what were "normal." When I explained to her that I was only coloring what was there, the colors that everyone could see on everybody and everything, she nearly had a cardiac arrest. Of course, it didn't occur to me that everyone didn't know all living things were colored on the outside. I learned later that these colors were auras and that I should keep my mouth shut. Lucky for me, I was a quick learner. I hastily announced that I was just trying to get attention and make Sister Carol's life miserable. It wasn't a moment too soon, either. My folks had planned to take me to a psychiatrist the very next day!

Catholic school also presented other problems.

I could not understand how I was made in the image and likeness of God, when I didn't look a thing like any of three— the Father was old, the Son had a beard, and the Holy Ghost looked like a bird. Why could a God who was "love" toss somebody into a bonfire for a small infraction such as eating meat on Good Friday? How could he sentence unbaptized children to purgatory instead of taking them into heaven? Or why would the pope think he possessed the red phone to God?

The biggest problem came one Sunday morning at church, just after the sermon. The priest announced that he was sending around a petition that the pope wanted us to sign. The gist of it was that birth control pills and abortion, "the heinous murder of babies," as the priest called it, should be outlawed without exception. It was the most ludicrous thing I'd ever heard. There were no allowances made for pregnant child rape victims or any other special circumstance.

Apparently, no one else in the church shared my view. There they were, all signing the petition without batting an eyelash. Finally, someone handed the clipboards to me. I gave it a once-over and passed it on to Mama.

Keeping Magick Alive

That was the day Dorothy washed her hands once and for all of the Catholic Church. Having to continue in this environment until she was old enough to get out on her own, Dorothy describes how she kept her magickal spirit alive.

Some of my spiritual turning points actually came in the form of birthday and Christmas gifts. First, there was a Ouija board. I played with it for hours, asking the same silly questions any other 13-year-old girl might ask: Would I be rich? Would I be a movie star? Who would I marry? I laughed at the answer to the last question: Jim Morrison. The Doors were hit-makers of the day, but years later, I actually did marry and divorce a man by that name! Everything went along splendidly until I finally confided to Mama that I could work the board all by myself, and then to squelch her disbelief, I showed her. Of course, the board mysteriously disappeared after that.

Help comes in many forms, and I guess its value is all in how you look at it. Some help was spiritually academic. It took on the guise of the cosmic workings and its magick, the Goddess Mysteries, and karmic law. I relished it, studied hard, and learned well.

Other help wasn't as much fun.

I learned that even though you could trust someone with your spiritual life, you might not be able to trust them with a blank check! Disheartening as it was, it was a lesson I never forgot.

The best help I ever received came one day when I was passing the window of a local bookstore. There it was: a book written just for me. It was *A Victorian Grimoire* by Patricia Telesco. I marched right in, bought the book, and then chuckled all the way home. It was obvious that the scripture-spouting salesclerk had no idea what was in her store or what she had sold me. Also, she had no way of knowing that by selling me that book, she had just changed my entire life.

My Link with Trish Telesco

Dorothy went home and immediately read the book—not just a chapter or two, but the entire thing! Afterwards, she did something she had never done before: She wrote a letter to the author.

Trish was already familiar to me because of *Circle Network News,* a quarterly newsletter that also had published some of my writings. Because of this, I felt I knew her, but still I felt a little silly writing the letter. No matter how hard I tried, I just couldn't stop myself. I mailed the letter that night. It never occurred to me that she might respond.

What ensued thereafter amounted to much more than a simple response from Trish. There was a flurry of letters between the two women and an embracing of each other's lives.

We somehow fell quickly into the deep and long-lasting sort of friendship it seems to take other folks years to develop. No matter what was wrong with one of us, the other seemed to have the answer. It was as if the Goddess had gifted me with Trish to supply a missing link I had previously been unaware of and, for that, I'll always be grateful.

Nowadays, Dorothy is grateful for a lot. She describes her office as brimming with mementos and symbols of links that the Goddess provided to help her along her way.

There's a book from Sirona Knight; a small hat ornament from Trish; cards and pictures from folks all over the country pinned helter-skelter on a bulletin board; feathers, stones, herbs, seashells, a cotton ball, and various other goodies here and there; and African violets, green plants, and Lego castles lining the walls. Somewhere in the middle are piles of Shadows screaming to be placed in binders and a desk that looks as though the latest hurricane has just blown through.

Sound like a mess? Maybe, but Dorothy claims that each and every item has special meaning, and together they track her progress as to what she has become, what she's accomplished, and the goals not yet reached. As a Wiccan High Priestess of the Georgian Tradition and a Witch for more than 20 years, Dorothy's office reflects the extraordinary progress of a small town southern belle, now an award-winning Wiccan author, who insisted she could change the world with a smile.

Being an Author—and Much More

When you write books, you wind up being a community leader of sorts, and that was a big shock to me. At the onset of my writing career, it never occurred to me that I would be a community leader. I began writing books because I communicate better on paper than I do verbally. The ancients played a great big trick on me, because now I get to run around and give speeches! That wasn't something I had anticipated, not in any manner. Recently, I was asked to join the New Millennium Council of American Witches, which is picking up where the old council left off in 1974. Right now, we are redefining Wicca and where we need to go from here.

One of Dorothy's goals as an author is to help shape people's spirituality in some fashion. She always writes her books based on her own experiences.

I would be a lousy research author. If I haven't been there, done that, and have the T-shirt, I don't really think I'm qualified to write it. Everything I write about I've tried at least twice to make sure I wasn't wrong the first time. I don't expect anyone to do something I either haven't done, or am not willing to try.

The first time my credentials were ever challenged by a former teacher, one of my friends said to me, "Congratulations, honey. You've just arrived." So whenever someone talks about me, or other Wicca authors, the way they do Crowley and Gardner, it means that we have done something. We have made a statement. The only people who never get talked about are the people who do nothing.

My View of the Future

I hope that religious practice will be much easier for my grandchildren than it is for us today, and that people will evolve toward more acceptance and tolerance of diversity. I think this is possible. In Goddess-oriented spiritualities, it's easier for other people to accept women's power. I personally love the idea of a goddess that watches over me and sees to it that I'm not going to fall over the edge of a cliff. She's been there, done that. A male God has no idea what menstrual cramps are like, what PMS is like, or what other things that women endure are like. I'm not just talking about physical things, but emotional things as well. It's really difficult to get close to a god that you know couldn't possibly understand how you feel.

Dorothy has experienced more positive than negative feedback from being an outspoken Witch in the 21st century.

Other than losing a job once, I really haven't had any negative experiences. I think everybody gets a few weird e-mails now and again. For the most part, I have been accepted as a part of mainstream America. Maybe that is because I expect people to accept me that way. It's part of my magick. I think we bring on our own negative stuff, so if you expect to be treated well, you will be.

Dorothy has high hopes that women will not only be empowered by the Goddess and by Wicca, but will also learn to wield their power wisely.

Power is a double-edged sword. You can use it to defend and protect, or you can use it to cut your own throat. I would like to see more Wiccans involved in their communities and in the greater organization in the movement. We need some sort of information packet for people who wind up in court and for people with jobs or custody of their children at risk. Education should come to the forefront, not Hollywood's education with movies such as *Hocus Pocus* or *The Witches of Eastwick*. That kind of education is ridiculous.

I would like to see Wiccans take a part in their communities and become a real part of them by doing things such as volunteering time at hospitals, nursing homes, and homeless shelters. We need to get involved and do some good work. I would like to see people take more of an interest in their Pagan Pride Day.

Image-Polishing

Right now, if Witches want to be seen, heard, and welcomed, it's important that we become more mainstream.

We don't want to look as though we just stepped off the set of the latest horror movie. More Wiccans are mainstream now. Those of us who dress mainstream are accepted in more mainstream arenas. I don't run around with a 5-inch pentagram around my neck and black makeup on. If we don't want people to perceive us as stereotypical Witches, then we need to take care not to look like the Hollywood stereotype. We need to do some image-polishing.

As Pagans, we cannot expect people to accept us as part of mainstream society unless we are out there doing things. We need to stay in touch with our government officials and find out what they are doing. We need to keep a check on how they are handling our lives.

As Pagans, we need to express our displeasure when it's necessary and we definitely need to vote. There is nothing that angers me more than that lackadaisical Pagan attitude. We need to pay attention or our rights are just going to fly right out the window. I would like to see people in the Wiccan movement speak at universities—not so much about our differences, but about our similarities.

Today, our strength is in our young people. They are the ones who are open-minded and more accepting. Eventually they will be the people who will be running this country, so it's important to educate them.

When I was 4 years old, I wanted to be famous. I really did! I don't know why, but I look back and I remember wanting to be really famous no matter what I did, but I didn't think I would be a Witch. It's funny, because now that I'm a famous Witch, I'm taken aback when someone recognizes me. It's an interesting twist of fate.

PATRICIA "TRISH" TELESCO

My most life-changing experience, which only happened recently, was finding a group of people, whom I call my tribe, in the greater magickal community. Discovering a group of people all over the United States with whom I have this amazing connection and sense of family is incredible. I never understood what community could mean until this group began to emerge in my life. Now I understand what it is to honor your tribes, love them, and keep them whole.

Patricia Telesco is one of the most prolific and active authors in the Wicca movement. She has written more than 40 books, including the best-selling A Charmed Life, A Witch's Beverages and Brews, Gardening With the Goddess, Goddess In My Pocket, *and* 365 Goddesses. *In addition, she is often on the road, giving*

*lectures and workshops, and doing readings and book
signings at book stores, festivals, and gatherings so much
so that she regards the people she meets at these magickal
events as special.*

My extended family includes the people I interact intimately with at festivals and gatherings. I find that going to these events refills my inner well, giving me the energy to keep writing and to come home to my children and husband refreshed. It also provides me with wonderful ideas for new books.

When I Knew I Was a Witch

When I think back to my childhood and see myself singing to trees, going to the forest for solace, and looking to the stars with hope, it appears I was always a Pagan at heart. I just didn't have a name for it until about 16 years ago.

*Wicca was the first spiritual philosophy Trish discovered
that mirrored what she had felt in her heart all along.*

Wicca was a good basic construct that provided ideas and form without blinders. I was totally surprised to find it through some local people. I never thought anybody with "outside-the-box" ideas lived in our neck of the woods.

*Spiritually, Trish came from of a very mixed-bag
background. Born as a Lutheran and having spent five
years in Pentecostal ministry, her sense of religion and
what it should be, or could be, wasn't clear.*

As I studied Wicca and global magickal/spiritual traditions, my vision of the potential in faith to change people's lives changed. It was very healing. It healed my relationship with Spirit.

Something Clicked

Trish's first exposure to an actual magickal procedure was an open circle she attended early in her quest.

The experience was as awkward as a three-antlered moose. It was interesting, kind of scary, and wholly foreign. I felt as if I'd been dumped in a different world without any frame of reference on which to draw, and without knowing the "lingo"—yet at the same time, it was oddly familiar and welcoming.

Something clicked inside my soul—something that woke up parts of my mind that frightened and confused me. It was something that wouldn't go away or be easily ignored. I remember that day as if it were only a second ago. I was talking to a friend who eagerly showed me an antique ring discovered at a flea market. The ring had tiny silver flowers and vines wrapped around the clear-cut amethyst as delicately as if they'd been grown by Nature herself. I reached to take a closer look.

Then, as I touched the stone, the world around me disappeared. I saw faces, people, and places that I didn't recognize. The occasion seemed sad, and then I knew why: A woman was in a casket, and her body bore the ring that I now held in my hand. My face turned white, I dropped the ring, and I quickly excused myself. I wondered what it was all about. Because I never did any type of psychedelic drugs in my life, perhaps this was the first sign of a real mental breakdown.

My husband Paul took me to see someone he knew named Dyane. She was a Cabbalist, someone trained in ancient ways of seeing and someone who practiced a form of magick. At that precise moment, I finally understood what it meant to literally feel torn in two directions. My mind reeled at this concept, but my heart yearned to know more. My heart won the argument with a hearty dose of logic mingled in that said, "What could it hurt?"

Dyane was charming and about Trish's height, with strawberry hair and fiery eyes.

She welcomed us with tea and hospitality. To this day, I thank Dyane for not pushing me that day, for not saying or asking too much too soon. She seemed to naturally sense my anxiety, and she handled it with uncommon grace, wisdom, and a wonderful knack for cooking. The plate filled with homemade sweets laid out neatly on an antique platter made it feel like a day at Grandma's.

When I Really Knew

It was then that they finally got to the moment of truth.

Dyane asked me to describe my experience in detail. As I did, she got the same funny smile on her face that I'd seen with Paul! Worse yet, she kept exchanging knowing glances with him, intense looks that bore a whole conversation without ever saying a word. What was this anyway—some kind of elite club where everyone knew a secret except me?

After I told my story, Dyane excused herself and retrieved a drawer full of beautiful, unique jewelry. She told me that many of the pieces were ones that she had brought with her from Israel. The others had been handed down or given as gifts.

The blank look on my face must have been humorous; it was obvious that I didn't take the cue, so she said to me, "I want you to pick up each one and tell me what you feel or see."

Dyane pointed emphatically, as if she were a determined mother who would not be moved. And even though I'd just met this woman, somehow I knew that this determination wasn't to be trifled with.

The next hour or so was an experience that defies explanation. I went through the jewelry one piece at a time, talking about various sensations and flashes that were coming to me unbidden. Truth be known, I felt totally foolish, but by the end of the "test," Dyane smiled at me warmly and told me that I was perfectly fine. She told me that I wasn't going crazy. She said, "There, there, dear…let me tell you about energy."

Trish discovered that Dyane was no intellectual slouch. She could talk about science and metaphysics and somehow make the two work together.

By the end of that day, my life was changed forever. The old axiom that "energy cannot be created or destroyed, but simply changes shape" had a whole new meaning in the face of psychic phenomena and magick.

In the ensuing days and months, Paul and Dyane continued to work patiently with Trish, along with a few other magickal friends who stumbled into their lives at just the right time.

These people were there to help birth and channel my psychic abilities, there to help me with astral attacks, and there to hold my hand when it all became too much for this naive young woman to handle alone. Coincidence? I don't think so. The Powers were nudging me in a specific direction and, for whatever reason, I was actually listening.

When, at last, the proverbial light bulb about spirituality and magick went on over my head in 1986, and things started making sense, a door also opened to me—actually, it blew off its hinges—and it remains gaping to this day.

When I Decided to Write

I never went looking to write for the New Age. It literally landed in my lap after a bout with chicken pox (I guess you could say I was itching to write). At that juncture I never expected a publisher to be interested in this self-dedicated, fly-by-the-seat-of-her-broomstick Witch. Fate had something else in mind, obviously—but that door would have remained firmly closed in my life if Wicca hadn't introduced itself to me and opened my mind to possibilities.

The Emergence of the Kitchen Witch

Trish is way beyond being out of the broom closet these days. She describes herself as a down-to-earth, militant, wooden spoon–wielding Kitchen Witch.

Mind you, I don't hang out a sign that says "Witch resides here" either. My faith is private, and if I choose to share it with someone that's fine. Similarly, if I choose not to, for whatever reason, that is also fine. I do think the magickal community needs to stand up and be counted, but there are times when wisdom must also prevail.

I prefer not to call Deity by any particular name. I designate it simply as Spirit. To me anything so vast and so above our mortal understanding should not be limited in my mind or my speech.

Regarding her connection with this deity, Trish confesses that her relationship is one of service.

More than a decade ago, I promised Spirit that I would give my hands and heart to the community for as long as it needed them. For me, magick is a way of thinking, living, and being. It is not something limited to a particular day, month, celebration, or gathering. Rather than practicing magick, I *am* the magick—24 hours a day, seven days a week.

One of the most empowering aspects of Wicca is that it encourages us to use our minds and hands. We should think about our faith, measure it against what can be proven, balance that with belief, and find a good middle ground. Similarly, we should work for what we desire because hard work is good magick. We shouldn't simply expect the universe to do it all for us. I think that Wicca encourages this practical foundation.

We're Here to Stay

Trish believes that the media may be our best ally in taking magickal traditions into the mainstream faiths.

I think anything that opens our minds just a little, anything that makes us laugh and realize that the old stereotype is just silly, anything that shows us helping others, is very good. Yes, these depictions are far from accurate, but on the other hand, that wouldn't sell, and we all know that business is business. Nonetheless, every person watching these shows, such as *Charmed* and *Sabrina,* is, at least indirectly, beginning to see that Wicca and magick aren't just a flash in the pan. We're here to stay.

Wicca is a Choice, Not an Edict

The mother of three children, Trish feels strongly about the future of Wicca and of humankind.

My children are being brought up to be good human beings—no dogma, no prayer, no preaching. If they show an interest in my spiritual path or my husband's path, we answer questions and let them try things. If they decide to peruse something, that is their choice. My eldest son considers himself agnostic. My little ones are busy experiencing the wonders of the world from the perspective of young minds. Is there magick in that? Of course. But I don't need to label it for them. They know!

Even after the many books she has written and the multitude of events at which she's appeared, when asked if she thinks she is a mover and a shaker in the Wiccan Movement, her response is still candid and witty.

A gentle nudger would be more like it. Although I have a voice that does get heard, I realize that I speak to a specific sector, and that's where my greatest interest lies. The other way I can use this nudge is by supporting specific Pagan projects such as land funds—and putting my author's seal of approval on those groups, events, and projects. To me, it's all about touching one life at a time and changing things one moment at a time. If I reach beyond that scope, I celebrate and thank Spirit for letting me help.

A. J. DREW

I do not think Witchcraft is going mainstream. I think mainstream is going Witchcraft. The ethics of Wicca are becoming the ethics of our society. Where Wicca teaches that animals have rights, U. S. law has started to recognize animal rights. Where Wicca teaches that all humans should have equal rights, U. S. law legislates against racism and sexism. Where Wicca teaches that "all acts of love and pleasure are my rituals," same-sex marriages are right around the corner. Everywhere we look, we are winning the battle against ignorance. Our ethics are becoming law.

An Urban Yeti

Author of Wicca For Men *and* Wicca Spellcraft for Men *and full-time owner of Salem West in Columbus, Ohio, A. J. often refers to himself as an urban yeti. A large, imposing, but soft-spoken man, he considered himself a patriotic Pagan. In fact, A. J. often holds the American flag high in a place of honor when he does public rituals.*

I have been Wiccan since I was about 14 years old, but I only realized I was a Witch after I opened a Pagan shop in a small town. You see, my childhood was a bit different from most. My mother was Catholic, my father Lutheran, my best friend Jewish, and my babysitter a Krishna. No one ever told me I had to be one or the other. When I discovered what is now commonly called Wicca, I found what I had always known: that the ultimate truth cannot be found in any one religion.

On Becoming Wiccan

I was trying to get laid. What else is on a 14-year-old boy's mind? I desperately wanted to get into the pants of a woman named Wanda. During one of my many efforts, she mentioned that she was learning about "The Old Religion" from a woman named Misty Lackey. I was an annoying child, so Misty didn't pay much attention to me, but I listened to everything Wanda related to me with anxious ears. Misty went on to be published as Mercedes Lackey, I think Wanda went on to become Catholic, and here I am telling my story in a book about Witches.

Initiation as Rebirth

Religious choice is just that: It is choice. Rather than attempting to follow a set of teachings that you do not believe in, you should pick the religion whose teachings reflect your own beliefs. In my case, those teachings are best described as Wicca.

I was introduced to the Old Religion when I was 13, and was initiated a couple of years later. (Initiations weren't generally conducted until the age of 18, for a variety of reasons.) My initiation wasn't anything as dramatic as what I have read in books. No knife was placed to my throat, and I was neither blindfolded nor tied hand to foot. Although the practice is rarely conducted today, at the time it was customary for women to initiate men and men to initiate women. To be honest, I have never found reference to my initiation in any of the many books I have read that address the issue, which is strange, because the format seemed very appropriate.

With no women present in the room, I was asked to lay down in the fetal position atop a throw rug with a rope tied to one end. The women entered the room and stood over the rope in a line. They separated their legs so that they had one foot on either side of the rope. I was told that "through woman you entered this world" by the first woman who stood directly before me. The men of the group pulled me, by the rope, through the tunnel that the women's legs had formed. I was pulled through the symbolic birth canal that the line formed. Once at the end, I was helped to my feet by our leader as she told me, "...and through woman you enter this circle." It was a different time. The word *circle* referred to the group more than an actual cast circle. The word *coven* was hardly ever used.

I know it seems a bit backwards, but prior to my initiation, I knew people in the circle only by their common or Pagan names. The next step in my initiation was to be introduced to each member more formally. My sponsor took me to each group member and introduced me by my birth name and the birth names of my mother and father. The format was: "I present to you Mr. John Smith, son of Ann Smith and Robert Smith." I was surprised to find that she had done her research, and I suspect that my surprise was well-intended. Each member replied with similar information, a welcome to the circle, and a gift. Most of the gifts were books. I felt more like a groom meeting his bride's parents than the initiate of a circle of Witches. The rest of the evening went the way a wedding reception would: We ate, we drank, and I had a truly wonderful time with my new kin.

Point, Counterpoint

As far as a life-defining situation, at the top is my contemplation of suicide and the experience of divine intervention. While living in Obetz, Ohio, I became very ill with a condition that attacked my lungs. It had gotten so bad that I could barely talk without losing my breath. I spent most of my time locked away in a small room with an air filter, a computer, and my rather large collection of guns.

The computer was my only connection to the outside world, so I spent hours each day reading and posting to news groups via local computer networks. One day, I spilled a bottle of Pepsi on the keyboard and flew into a rage. At the time, keyboards were very expensive, and I had just destroyed the only method I had to remain sane. I started cursing the keyboard for not having a membrane to protect it, myself for being so clumsy, and even the Pepsi for being wet and sticky. I eventually cursed the Creator for giving me the desire to be active but allowing my lungs to be attacked by the illness. My damaged lungs could not keep up with the yelling. By screaming out loud, I expended what little oxygen my lungs were able to send into my bloodstream. I fell to my knees on the floor and cursed the Creator for giving me all of my dreams and then robbing me of the ability to fulfill them by making me so sick.

Then I saw my shotgun resting in the corner just a few feet away. I considered taking my own life. It would have been so easy. Mission unsuccessful, abort and try again. But just as quickly as the idea came into my head, something happened. As quickly as the thought of suicide entered my mind, a counterpoint challenged my self-destruction. I like to think that counterpoint was Goddess. In an instant, I understood every portion of the universe, my purpose, and the purpose of every grain of sand. Unfortunately, I forgot most of it. I don't know if I passed out or hallucinated due to oxygen and sleep deprivation, but it seemed as though for one absolutely lucid moment, I understood everything there is to understand in the universe. I also experienced an incredible feeling of dread, as if I had just fallen love and my love left for a long business trip. Unfortunately, that lucid moment passed quickly and I returned to my normal self.

What A. J. did manage to remember from this extraordinary experience changed his life.

I had the very strange understanding that if I wanted to live, I had to support life. I sold most of my extensive gun collection, became a vegetarian, opened a Pagan shop, and started making plans to host a festival that would make a difference in my community. I wanted other Pagans to understand the feeling that I had been given in that instance. My medical condition went into full remission. The bumper sticker that reads "Born-Again Pagan" has a very special meaning for me.

Wiccan Defines What I've Become

I cannot recall a point in my life where I was definitively not Wiccan. I grew into this religion and it grew into me. I did not take on the title Wiccan and then transform my life into what someone said a Wiccan life should be. Instead, I became the person that I am over the course of my life, and the word *Wiccan* best fits that which I have become.

For A. J., it was an army chaplain who first used the word to describe his religious beliefs.

I had placed the word *Pagan* on the paperwork for my dog tags. Those tags came back saying *No Preference*. I brought this to the attention of my drill sergeant, who sent me to the chaplain. The chaplain asked me what my belief structure entailed. I explained and he told me that I was Wiccan. Although I argued that the term Wiccan was reserved for elders, I was only a low-ranking Army private. The military had other ideas. Per the chaplain's instructions, the word *Wicca* was placed on my dog tags. When I returned to the United States from overseas, I discovered that many people had taken on the title as a result of Scott Cunningham's book, *Wicca: A Guide for the Solitary Practitioner.*

I think of the word *Witch* much in the same way I think of the word *nigger*. It is a word used by people who seek to repress a race and used by members of repressed races to rob the thunder from their oppressors. Again, it wasn't until opening my store that I felt the oppression that is associated with such words.

Magick Is Natural and Automatic

I count myself as a member of the Creation's Covenant tradition of Wicca. However, I do not hold any of the pre–Burning Times lineage fantasies that seem to come with the word *tradition*. My favorite Divine are Lord Shiva and Lady Pavarti. When doing works, I have had much better luck trying to destroy disease than I have had trying to heal a body. (This gives insight into why Lord Shiva is my preferred God archetype, as he is the Hindu god of creation and the embodiment of masculinity.)

I cannot remember a day that has come and gone without my use of magick. It can be something as simple as hoping the electric bill is low as I open it, or sprinkling black salt outside my home to keep bad neighbors away. Or it can be more complex. Either way, I am not really the type to get spooky. Magick is natural and automatic. We can choose to use it consciously or continue to muddle through our lives using magick, often accidentally, to our detriment. Consider self-doubt and the magickal teaching that like attracts like.

The most empowering aspect of Wicca is that two seemingly opposite beliefs can both be true. One of the underlined principles in the Wiccan religion is that what is right for one person is not necessarily right for the next. My Catholic mother and I do not have to agree on the format of our religion to be completely confident that we are both doing what is right. With this concept, my support base is not as limited as that of someone who is homophobic, racist, or sexist. I can be Wiccan and have no doubt that I will visit my mother in heaven and she will visit me in summerland.

The people of my coven are my family. I do not buy into the idea of artificial covens. The idea of bringing people together based only on their religion is probably the most common root of organizational failure. Your people are your people regardless of either blood or religious preference.

How Others See Me

Despite his high profile, A. J. indicates that he has encountered very little prejudice.

Other than the year in which my Pagan shop was in a very small town, I have had very few experiences in which I felt I was accepted differently due to my religion. I simply do not share my religion with everyone I meet. No giant pentagram belt buckles here. I believe those who later scream, "Persecution!" are the ones who generate the great majority of problems. This is sad when you consider the amount of real persecution in the world.

I did have a landlord once say that he did not want to rent commercial space for my store because he did not like the idea of having such an establishment on his property. As far as I am concerned, the property is his, so he can do with it what he will.

The Real Witches Ball

A. J. Drew has a very bold and straightforward approach to Wicca and its practices, as evidenced by the Real Witches Ball, a weekend event that he hosts and organizes in Columbus, Ohio, every year just before, or on, Samhain. Now in its ninth annual installment, the Real Witches Ball continues to grow larger and larger, with thousands of Pagans in attendance. That's pretty remarkable for an idea that came from one lucid moment.

After I opened Salem West, I started making plans to host a Pagan festival that would make a difference, and that was how the Real Witches Ball began. The first Real Witches Ball was held the same year I opened my store, but it was so small that no one really noticed. The second was a bit larger, and today we have started looking at places to move it to because we have just about outgrown the facilities in our neighborhood. Although I think it is a few years off, the ultimate goal is to create a Pagan community responsible for hosting and planning The Real Witches Ball and festivals for each of the High Days.

The Real Witches Ball is an "in-town" Pagan event. It is a time when just about all of the stores, bars, and other establishments in the Garden District of Columbus, Ohio, transform the neighborhood into a Pagan wonderland. People check in at my store, Salem West (1209 North High Street), and they get a program detailing the events that take place during the Ball, all within walking distance of each other.

The reason for the Ball is that education and revelry are in high demand. Sure, you can read a book about the Pagan community, but that absolutely cannot replace personal contact with those of like minds. By day, the Real Witches Ball is back-to-back and overlapping workshops offered by some of today's cutting-edge authors, community leaders, and leading educators. We have honored guests such as authors Sirona Knight, Dorothy Morrison, Patricia Telesco, and M. R. Sellars. By night, the Ball is probably one of the single best places to meet those of like minds. Be it in the drum circles, at the workshops and rituals, or in the taverns, there is always something at the Ball to raise your smile.

PHYLLIS CURROT

To practice Wicca, you need to get out of the living room and go outside, even if you have to climb onto the roof of your apartment building. You can't practice Wicca disconnected from Divinity and the embodiment of Divinity.

I have a country house where I do my writing. It's on the north fork of Long Island and it's an ecosystem unto itself. It's farm country, and the old potato farms are being replanted with grape vines. As I sit here looking out the window, I see creek with swans. Out the other window are two crows. We are raised with this transcendent God belief that he's not present in the world, and that's what keeps us in our living rooms and in our heads instead of in our bodies and the body of experience.

The Earth is the embodiment of divinity, and Nature is our teacher. We all have the same teacher. It's one reason I'm such an advocate for people getting out of their heads and into their bodies, into the body of the Divine, into Nature. Wicca is all about feeling, and not a head trip. It's a journey of the heart.

Religion Wasn't Part of my Vocabulary

Phyllis Currot's first book, Book of Shadows: A Modern Woman's Journey into the Wisdom of Witchcraft and the Magick of the Goddess, *propelled her into the public eye as a prominent Witch in the Wiccan Movement. It tells of her personal journey from being an Ivy League lawyer to becoming a Witch in New York City.*

There are people who know they are Witches as children, but I wasn't one of them. I was clearly set on the path, but I don't think my parents intended it. One of my absolute favorite books as a child was the original *The Wizard of Oz*, where Dorothy literally walks through the four directions on her journey to discover that she had the power within her all along. We would get to the end of the book, and I would always say, "Start over." I now have a cairn terrier, and he looks like a blonde Toto from *The Wizard of Oz*.

My mother used to read to me before bed every night. Besides *The Wizard of Oz*, she also read me *Bulfinch's Mythology*, cover to cover. I was raised in a very intellectual household, not a religious one. Religion wasn't part of my vocabulary. It was perceived as superstitious, something that impeded people from fulfilling themselves, a way of controlling people as opposed to liberating them. I still think that is largely true.

The Attraction of Nature

Even though she was raised in the suburbs and went to schools in the city, the country was always an important part of Phyllis's upbringing.

When I was young, I went to camp. My mother took us on weekend expeditions out into beautiful and natural areas, to Maine, Vermont, the Berkshires, the Catskills, and the ocean. As a child, I always had a feeling of happiness and joy and presence, of not being alone when I was in the woods. I think that is true for most children. We are just weaned away from it by a very repressive culture.

Phyllis's attraction to the country and to Nature set the stage for her attraction to Wicca.

It was a fascinating series of experiences for me. The path really opened up during my second year of law school, when all sorts of remarkable things started happening simultaneously. I was very fortunate, because those experiences had an objective part to them. You don't need to be psychic or have special powers to be a Witch. My definition of a Witch is someone who is paying attention—someone who is able to see the Sacred in the world, to see its patterns in play in their own lives.

The Journey Into Wicca

Phyllis's journey into Wicca began when she was in her early 20s.

I realized that I wasn't going nuts, but I knew there was more to reality than what meets the eye, so I turned to physics. I was hyper-rational. I had gotten a philosophy degree at Brown and a law degree at New York University. When I turned to physics, I got the explanation that everything is energy and interconnected, and that the mind has the capacity to interact with the universe on that quantum level in very profound and amazing ways. This gave me an explanation as to why I was having premonitions that manifested and dreams that came true, as well as why my senses became very acute.

The most profound thing that happened was a recurring dream. I probably had it five times. It was a very vivid dream. I would wake up from it, which is how I remembered it. It was a simple and enigmatic. In the dream, I saw a woman who was somewhat larger than life with a crown on her head. She was seated, bare-breasted, and holding a book in her hand. She was very serious and maternal, but not severe. As I looked at her, a light grew at her throat. It would get brighter and brighter, the dream would bleach out, and I would wake up. Sometimes when I woke up, she would still be visible, and other times it would just be white. I had no idea what that was.

Phyllis was having a series of experiences of Dionysus manifesting at the same time and was hearing pan piping.

I had the good sense to follow the sound of the music, and through a series of synchronicities, I was led to a coven of Witches. I was offered an opportunity to have my tarot cards read by someone who described herself as a White Witch. I had read tarot cards in high school, but no one had ever read my cards for me.

The White Witch asked me what my question was, and I responded, "Where does my path lie?" I really wanted to understand what was happening, and I wanted to keep experiencing it. I wanted it to make sense.

She replied, "It lies within."

Without hesitating, I asked, "Yeah, but how do I get there?" I had always been a social activist, and my family was made up of political activists and union organizers. My mother was an activist working with the NAACP in the early 1930s, so I was very outward-oriented toward social justice, not toward the inner path.

I didn't really know what the White Witch meant. When she was done reading my cards, she said she was starting a

women's group and thought I might find the answers I was
looking for there. She suggested I come. I thanked her, but I
had no intention of going.

A Special Opportunity

*At the time, Phyllis was managing a rock 'n' band and
working as a lawyer. A couple weeks passed, and Phyllis
received a phone call. It was the White Witch.*

She told me I was given a very special opportunity. There
were precious few covens in the 1970s. Everything was secret,
and even if you went into an occult shop, it was impossible to
get invited into a circle. There were very few books. Nothing.
I had no sense of how amazing it was because I had no sense
of *what* it was.

*About the same time as these events were unfolding,
Phyllis was spending a lot of time at the Metropolitan
Museum of Modern Art.*

I was always drawn to the Egyptian collection. I was walking through the museum, trying to figure out a lot of personal
decisions one day. I wasn't thinking about this circle, and I
found myself in an enclosed sculpture garden that was new, a
place I had never been in before. I was strolling through it,
and suddenly I was confronted by the figure in my dream. It
was a statue called the Libyan Sybil that was sculpted in Rome
by an American sculptor. It was she. The bleaching out from
my dream happened, and I almost passed out. A guard came
over and sat me down. I felt nauseous; I couldn't even look at
her. There was a six-pointed star at her throat and a crown on
her head. She was holding a sheaf of paper. I was blown away,
and I looked up the word Sybil. It said, "Ancient Priestess -
Witch." This circle I had been invited to was the last place I
had wanted to go, but I went.

When people enter altered states of consciousness, they can more easily interact with the quantum field of the universe in a seemingly magickal way. This was what happened to Phyllis.

I wasn't living in California; there weren't any Native Americans to study with, no Esalan, nothing. I hadn't taken drugs before, so I didn't really have a frame of reference for mystical experiences. I couldn't argue with what I had just experienced in the sculpture garden. It was a life-changing experience.

An Inauspicious Beginning

Phyllis's first ritual experience was initially extremely uncomfortable.

There were about 75 women at the back of the bookstore in a room that you got to by way of a secret door. The back room was a temple. There were no green faces, warts, or pointy hats, just a lot of very cool women from their late teens to white-haired ladies. It was utterly amazing. My friend went with me, and there were some people there who were waiting for me to come. The coven's Crone welcomed me.

Phyllis was comfortable with the women of the coven, but she wasn't comfortable with the ritual.

I had no idea what they were doing. They had an altar in the middle and were saying all kinds of things that made no sense to me. Then they walked around the four directions and said things that made no sense to me. I didn't have the faintest idea what they were doing. They talked about the Goddess, and at the time, I couldn't even imagine God, let alone the bigger stretch to Goddess, but I was intrigued. My experiences had been so profound that I wanted to understand what they were, and I wanted to explore them. I wanted to keep having them.

At that very first ritual, Phyllis was told that Witches had nothing to do with Satanists. That was a distortion that had arisen in the Witch craze and an extension of the Inquisition.

Because part of my family is Jewish, I had a sensitivity for what these women were saying. It rang true for me. I went out and did my research, and it was indeed true. Wicca has absolutely nothing to do with Satanism or those wacky stereotypes. The accusations against Witches are similar to the accusations made against Jews. The stereotype of the big-nosed Jew and the big-nosed Witch, the hooves, the horns, the worshipping of Satan, the murdering of Christian babies, the same distortion, same lies, same torture—but aimed at women, many of whom were not Witches.

It was during the Burning Times that women lost their entire standing. It was the female holocaust, the historical moment when women lost their place within the culture. Women couldn't own or inherit property. They were forbidden from receiving an education, and they couldn't leave their houses. It's why we have the struggle today for equal rights for women, to control our own bodies, and to participate in the culture.

The Minoan Sisterhood

Phyllis started to work with these women and stayed with it for three and a half years. There were two Gardnerian priestesses who decided they wanted to do a women mysteries circle. They called it the Minoan Sisterhood.

The two priestesses were Italian American, working class, and salt-of-the-earth. They both gave the most minimal explanations for everything. They showed me how to do what they knew how to do. That is one of the reasons I am still an advocate for Wiccan practices as a methodology for encountering the Divine and making magick.

Other women began pressing her to do a circle, so Phyllis started a coven and has now been working in one for almost 20 years.

I now work with men and women. If someone had asked me in high school what I wanted to be when I grew up, I would never have anticipated being a Witch. But it makes perfect sense. It's a profound spiritual path. I call my tradition the Shamanic Wicca tradition. My work has its Gardnerian roots, but they are adapted and very deconstructed.

Mistrusting Organized Religion

The question about the empowering aspects of Wicca brings out Phyllis's basic distrust of organized religion.

In Wicca, there is no prophet, no guru, and no hierarchy; everyone who practices the religion of Wicca is creating it. It is a new religion. I do not believe that what we are doing is what was being done 600, or even 50, years ago. In fact, the single most significant event in any culture throughout history has been the birth of a new religion, and that is what Wicca is. That's part of its strength.

Phyllis believes that when people truly learn to master Wiccan practices then the practices will transform them.

If they play-act, which you can do with Witchcraft, and mouth other people's words and not actually engage the practices, then they are going to stay on the surface of the experience. That's one of the reasons I wrote my second book, *Witch Crafting: A Spiritual Guide to Making Magic.* It's not a how-to book; it's a why-do book.

The Path I've Chosen

Each person has a different role in life, depending on the path we choose.

I've always been a forward thinker, so I've been working on deconstructing Wiccan dogma. I start out by saying that if I don't tick somebody off, then I'm not doing my job right. I have very specific criticisms of how contemporary Wicca is being practiced.

For one thing, lots of people who are coming into Wicca recently and basing their practices on the literature that has been published are approaching magick in a very mechanistic fashion. In keeping with the need for instant gratification in our culture, they see spellcasting as the most important aspect of Wicca. So then people see Wicca not as a religion, but as a means for manipulating the universe. In order to secure the goodies, they want the magick spell and word. The whole idea of "just give me the spell, give me the formula, tell me where to stand, what to say, and what to grind up and burn"— that whole view comes from the modern rationalist view. It's the idea that the universe is a machine and that all you need is the right fuel or ingredients.

The universe is not a machine; it's an organic entity. It is holy, sacred, and alive.

The other bugaboo I have with contemporary Wiccan practice is the Threefold Law. My specialty in philosophy was ethics, and from the very beginning the Threefold Law drove me mad. It is not a basis for ethics, and it's certainly not a basis for Wiccan ethics. It is essentially a theory of punishment. It's patriarchal. It's saying, "I won't hurt you, because if I hurt you something much worse will happen to me. So I will behave and be good."

Every time I read an article on Wicca, it seems that every Witch in the universe is saying that we don't do bad things because we believe that what we do is returned to us three times, and I cringe. The press prints that and never questions it, because it is in keeping with the Judeo-Christian model that if you behave badly you will be punished.

The Threefold Law was just a manifestation in the 1960s from the whole Eastern Karma thing. If we are going to have a basis for ethics in shaping a new religion and taking responsibility for shaping a new religion that has the potential for changing the world in the ways that it most needs it, we need to look very carefully at bases for our own morality, for our choices, and for the way we conduct ourselves.

For me, the theory of punishment is not the basis for how I make my decisions and behave in the world. It comes from the old biblical model.

Our morality as Witches comes from the fact that we live in a world that is sacred. As Witches, we are paying attention to the fact that the world we live in is sacred. It's holy and divine, so the only way to behave in a world that is charged with divinity is with reverence, respect, and gratitude.

Even when you are dealing with people who are dreadful and horrible, there is an understanding that there is an underlying divine energy. Nature shows us that we have to defend ourselves. You don't find evil in Nature, but you do find it in humanity. From that patriarchal model that God placed man here on Earth to have dominion over all things, people engage in evil because they are disconnected from the Divine.

What Is the Magick?

Life is magick in its purest form. What is the magick in Phyllis's life?

The common definition is that magick is the art of changing consciousness at will, which I think is far too narrow. It's a useful beginning point in that we need to shift our consciousness to see the Sacred.

But magick is not just the changing of consciousness to project your will to manifest your desire, and it's not just formulas, spells, and potions. Magick isn't something you do to the world.

Magick is something that the divinely living universe does to you. It is a partnership, a co-creative process, an artwork, and a fulfillment of destiny, which is full of difficulty, challenge, struggle, and hardship.

It's not about instant gratification, but it is about ecstasy.

What Is a Witch?

To Phyllis, a Witch is somebody who has learned to use Wiccan practices.

The practices enable you to take off the blindfold and see the Sacred—in yourself, others, and the world. Once you have made that connection, that's when the magick starts. Your life becomes magickal. Making magick, casting spells, and creating rituals becomes not a way of manipulating, but of creating, not a way of commanding and controlling, but of communing and co-creating. Magick has always been distinguished from religion, and I think that's false. When you and the universe are dancing together, when you are creating together, you make magick. You see the world in a totally different way. I practice Wicca by always expressing my appreciation to the Divine. The Sacred is present in the world and in all people, and that's where the magick comes from.

The Healing Work of Wicca

Much of what Wiccans do is healing work—for themselves, others, and the Earth. The Goddess energy is very much a healing energy. We know from experiments that have been conducted and studies that have been published by Duke University and other universities that people who don't know that they have been prayed for, by people they don't know, have a significantly higher survival rate than people who aren't prayed for. When you practice Wicca, you realize that everything is interconnected.

I have two very good friends, both of whom are Witches and one of whom is a member of my group. Both were diagnosed with terminal illnesses. I'm a big advocate of using everything at your disposal: traditional medical protocol enhanced with herbs, acupuncture, diet, visualization, and magick. Both of these people were supposed to be dead within two years, and it's been 10. Periodically, the entire community has sent healing energy to them, and we regularly put one of them in the center of the circle, do visualizations, and run energy through him. We mostly do laying on of hands and moving energy. We invoke gods and goddesses of healing and raise energy from the Earth. We begin by connecting to the Divine always, and then we direct the energy, in this case, toward healing.

One of the most profound experiences Phyllis has had with healing was her own healing.

Most everyone who walks this path in a serious way has to confront the dynamic of becoming ill. I didn't think that when I was young. Wicca is an initiatory path, not a path where we fly to heaven, but a subterranean path. It has always been an Earth religion where we go down and through and then come back up.

I became extremely ill, and I was dying. I had picked up two very obscure parasites. It took almost 13 years to diagnose them and by that time, they were pre-cancerous. I had the metabolism of an 80-year-old woman, and I couldn't stand without leaning on something. My blood pressure was appalling. It was awful.

I had gotten one of the parasites in Costa Rica while I was producing a documentary. I picked up the second on my honeymoon in Italy in the Bay of Naples, at the site of the ancient temple of the Cumayan Sybil, who was the Sybil devoted to Hecate. The site had been built by the Goddess-worshipping Minoans, so everything fit into place.

I realized that I had been initiated by Hecate. I felt as if I had been living in the Underworld. I had to make the journey back and was able to heal and come back as a result of the discovery of the spiritual dynamics of why and where I had gotten sick. It was part of my initiation.

Dealing with Family and the Public

I was very open with my family and took my time explaining Wicca to them little by little. My mother was always a feminist, so she appreciated the feminist point of view. I don't think my parents ever understood the spiritual aspects, although they were both two of the most spiritual people I have ever known. The rest of my family all know I'm a Witch. I have always been ahead of the curve, but I think they were all kind of stunned that I could do this in such a public and visible way.

Most of my law business has gradually disappeared. I also had a real-estate practice with lots of very traditional, conservative, long-term, male clients who sort of evaporated after my first book was published.

I still have female clients. When I went public, I lost a lot of very lucrative aspects of my law practice, so it was a sacrifice. But in exchange for that sacrifice, I've been given the chance to do what I love most. I have discovered that I love to write, lecture, and travel all over the world.

I was nervous when I went public—and scared to death about what was going to happen. I got some flack from my male colleagues with the standard jokes and put-downs. I had experienced a similar sort of patronizing behavior when I first went to law school. At that time, 5 percent of lawyers were women. What I experienced when I went public was reminiscent of my law school experience, so I was better able to deal with it. I knew the problem was other people's and not mine.

I get hate mail periodically. As a lawyer, I have always been public. I have a P. O. box and sometimes get pamphlets about Witches being Satanists. I keep them because, at one point, I was getting threatening phone calls. I received a death threat during my book tour in Boulder, Colorado, and I had to change hotels.

You have to be prepared to fight a battle, and you have to be prepared to pay the price. I made the choice and paid the price. Because of my willingness to pay the price, I won the great prize: the freedom from fear and the ability to do what I love most in life. The farther away you get from the machine, the easier you can find your authentic self.

Wiccan writers and activists many times do what they must, driven by their deep desire to make the world a better place to live, particularly in terms of religious and spiritual freedom. This desire keeps them moving forward, often in the face of obstacles, dangers, and pressures.

If you are going to be public and fight this battle, you have to be smart. You have to understand that people perceive you through a distorted lens. If you are going to assume the responsibility of being a Wiccan activist, you have to do it by understanding that part of your responsibility is to make a correction for the distortion in their lens. That requires you to be a shapeshifter.

There is nothing about Witchcraft that requires us to wear black robes. That's not a part of my religion. Dressing that way plays into society's stereotypes. If you are going to be an advocate for the Wiccan community in mainstream culture, you have to do so in a way that is effective. To me, that means you have to present the best aspect of who we are.

When I'm in public, I don't wear black robes. I wear a business suit when I do an interview. Instead of seeing someone who frightens them because I look like a stereotypical Witch, people see that I look the way they do. They are more able to listen and hear what I have to say.

We deserve to practice our religion in peace. We have children, and we have to protect them from persecution. We should be able to practice our religion and not be afraid of losing our jobs or custody of our children. That means that we have a lot of very hard work to do to normalize our reception. We have to correct the negative stereotype.

Wicca and the Mainstream

Phyllis has done a lot to bring Wicca into the mainstream. She has been extremely visible in the media and very outspoken.

I was never a person who sought the public eye. I have a unique position where I can interface between the Wiccan community and the mainstream, between the community and the media. I hired the top public relations person in the United States, the same person who works with Deepak Chopra and Marianne Williamson. I spent a fortune putting money into the effort of being highly visible. We mounted a campaign that had never been done before on television, on the radio, and in major magazines and newspapers—and not just in this country, but around the world in places such as London, Sydney, and Amsterdam.

With the rarest exception, the campaign was absolutely positive. Even the *National Enquirer* ran a positive piece on Wicca. I like to think that the campaign actually made a difference, because there has been a key change in the amount of coverage Wicca is getting and the quality of that coverage and respect. Had I attempted this 10 years ago, it wouldn't have worked.

Into the Future

If you work these practices, they render results. I'm a rationalist, and magick works. I think that is why so many people are drawn to it. We are hungry to be in the presence of divinity. We have been without for so long, it's become a hunger of our souls. There is a wound at the center of the Western world, and there is a tremendous need for that divine connection.

As Wicca goes mainstream, Wiccans are accepted more and more. People come to Wicca and find that it works. Because it works, they stay, and more people come with them (for example, husbands, brothers, sisters, friends, parents, and children). It's not an abstract religion based on fate or dogma. It connects you to the Divine and renders positive results.

Because Wicca is such a powerful spirituality, it terrifies the powers that be. Since the 2000 election, there has been an acceleration of legal cases due to the brazenness of Christian groups trying to assert their power. I do a lot of interface work, sometimes at very high levels. Every week, I get two or three e-mails from people that are fired from their jobs because they are Wiccan.

Phyllis, like many other Wiccan authors, truly believes that the Wiccan Movement offers the things that the world most needs at this critical moment.

We are living *The Lord of the Flies.* We are exploiting the Earth for short-term greed. That's what you get when God isn't present. The question is: How do we change that?

I believe we can change it by rediscovering the Sacred. You can find the Sacred in yourself, in your life, in Nature, in the world, and in other people. When you do find it, you start to live in a world that is literally charged with divinity. When you see and experience the world in that way, it changes everything about the way in which you live. You don't have to think twice about recycling or living in a way that is respectful of the Earth. It creates the posture to live in a way that is healthy and balanced and that will save us from ourselves.

6
RAVEN GRIMASSI

I think the absence of teachings that instill shame and low self-esteem is among the most empowering aspects of Wicca. Wicca encourages the inherit goodness in individuals and promotes self-worth. Wicca teaches that the divine spark of our creators dwells within us and that each person is valuable, is worthy, and has his or her own unique beauty as a result.

Magick is another aspect that is empowering. Magick awakens the ability to make changes in your life and to live life not as a victim, but as a participant. In Wicca, there are neither entities nor people to blame; Wicca teaches that we are ultimately responsible for the situations we find ourselves in, and we must take the steps to alter our course.

Raven Grimassi is the award-winning author of The Wiccan Mysteries *and* The Encyclopedia of Wicca and Witchcraft, *as well as the publisher and editor of*

Raven's Call, *a journal of modern Wicca, Witchcraft, and magick. He is also the owner of Raven's Loft in Escondido, California, a Pagan store dealing in the "quaint and curious." Italian by birth, he seeks his spirituality through his heritage, which includes a deep connection to the Earth.*

The "Ways" I Learned Growing Up

When he was much younger, Raven clearly understood that there were differences between himself and other kids.

It was almost always apparent, from a very young age, that I was not like the other kids. I was interested in looking for Fairies while my friends were catching frogs and lizards to play with. My earliest memories are of my mother working in her garden and calling me over to join her. She would say, "Did I ever tell you what we do with this herb?" It was there in her garden that I learned the lore of plants and the magick that unites us with everything else on the Earth.

All of this was simply "what we do," and it wasn't formally called anything other than the "ways" until I reached puberty. It wasn't until age 13 that I knew *Witchcraft* was the word for the ways I had learned growing up.

In the Summer of 1969, I encountered a woman who worked in an herb shop in the Old Town district of San Diego that specialized in herbal teas and carried a wide selection of bulk herbs. She commented on the unusual collection of herbs I purchased and remarked that they would not be used to make tea. I replied, "No, I don't use them for tea," and she interjected, "No, but they would make interesting incenses."

After several more visits to the herb shop—and many more cryptic conversations—one day she invited me to return at closing time. Shortly after my arrival, she showed me an altar in the back of the shop. It was similar in many ways to the type of altar I was taught to set. She went on to tell me that she practiced Wicca and explained that this was an old word for Witchcraft. This was the first time I encountered anyone outside of my family line who practiced Witchcraft.

First Encounters

My first magickal experience was due solely to my own actions. It occurred when I raised some small waves on a perfectly still lake while performing an ad-lib (some might say intuitive) chant. It was a profound experience because I did not think it would work! This was in my teen years.

My first formal solo spell was performed when I was in my early teens, and it was an attraction spell designed to draw a particular girl's attention. I raised energy through chanting and I asked the gods to allow the magick to work so that I would be given a second look. I used a barbecue to burn herbs as an offering to the Moon Goddess, and I marked out a pentagram, large enough to stand in, with five candles.

My actual journey into Wicca had more to do at first with trying to be with like-minded people closer to my own age. Wicca has many things in common with Italian Witchcraft, so the transition was much easier and more comfortable than it might have been had I not already been acclimated to the Craft.

The woman who managed the herb shop in San Diego introduced me to a gentleman who worked at a bookstore in Pacific Beach. After several visits and many lengthy chats, he introduced me to a woman that went by the name Lady Heather. It was she who eventually initiated me into Wicca. I think in some ways I was as much enchanted by her good looks as I was by the promise of embracing Wicca, but, then again, I was quite young in those days.

In time I came to love the ways of Wicca and the people with whom I associated. It quickly moved beyond the friendships I formed and into a spiritual place. Wicca, for me, always felt like a home away from home. I loved the gentleness of the gods and the people with whom I circled. Lady Heather claimed to be an initiate with lineage back to Gerald Gardner. Over the years, I came to view the material she taught as a blend of Gardnerian and Alexandrian.

A Mysterious Initiation

Raven's first experience with initiation outside of Italian Witchcraft was, in many ways, similar to the Wiccan initiations into other traditions he experienced in later years.

The initiation process began with me arriving, as agreed, on the night of the full moon at the home of the High Priestess. There were only four coven members in attendance that night. I was taken into a back bedroom by a young woman and told to remove my clothing, which I did. She returned shortly with a candle in a holder and set it on the bed stand. I was directed to watch the flame burn until someone came to get me.

I watched the candle burn and listened to the odd sound coming from somewhere in the house. Eventually I felt the setting pass away. I could have been anywhere, in any time period.

Eventually, the same woman appeared and blindfolded me. She then tied both of my hands behind my back and attached the rope to one of my ankles. After this, she escorted me to the edge of the ritual circle in another room of the house. The smell of incense greeted me and heightened my awareness. The glow of candles could be discerned through my blindfold. The setting was quite mysterious.

The initiation ceremony itself felt "soft" in some way, as though the air around me was made of wisps of cotton. Part of the ritual was designed to create apprehension, but I did not feel apprehensive.

Much of the ritual was similar to other experiences I had in Italian Witchcraft, and I believe this is one of the reasons why it lacked a certain intensity. However, the rite was moving and inspiring in a manner of its own.

Once the ceremony was complete, the ritual turned into a welcoming party. We all talked and drank wine into the early hours of the morning.

Encountering More Wiccan Traditions

Another tradition I was initiated into is called the Brittic tradition. The High Priest and High Priestess claimed it was an old system, blending Basque Witchcraft and English Wicca. It differed from other traditions primarily in the use of a "secret language" to cast the ritual circle, among other uses.

I first became involved with this group when I attended an open discussion night. I returned several times and made friends with some of the other seekers. The High Priest and High Priestess were very nice folks, and I came to hold much affection for them. They eventually brought up the question of initiation, and I was eager to belong to another coven. After several months, I was initiated into the Brittic system.

Curiously, the couple disappeared several months later. They moved away with no notice, and I never heard from them again. I continue to cling to the notion that their disappearance had nothing to do with me personally. I retained a friend from the coven who eventually became a student of mine.

After this, I created my own system and put together a coven called the Coven of Sothis. It was an eclectic system of Witchcraft that eventually disbanded, with some of the members joining a magickal society.

I later created the Order of the Sacred Path. Sometime around 1983, I was initiated into the Pictish-Gaelic tradition by a friend. He claimed the system was a hereditary Witchcraft tradition that was in danger of disappearing, because the elders were all passing away due to old age. I agreed to become a guardian of the material and accepted initiation in order to have the right to possess the material.

One of the curious things about this system is that prior to initiation, just hearing the names of the deities always made me feel very dizzy and sleepy. This happened on several occasions, but following initiation it never happened again.

Eventually, I returned to the practice of Italian Witchcraft, which is my sole focus now. The tradition is now called the Arician Ways, and we have members throughout the United States, as well as one in Australia. The main covenstead is located at Crow Haven Ranch, a four-acre ranch nestled in an isolated rural setting in southern California. We have built a permanent stone circle in an oak grove on the property and have attempted to re-create the Sacred Grove of Diana at Lake Nemi there. Many people have felt the vibration of the Old Ways that now resonates in the grove.

Wicca Changed my Life

The earliest life-changing experience was the demise of my first marriage, due largely to the increasing openness of my practice of Witchcraft. From this I learned the price for living one's truth.

Second only to this, as a life-changing experience, was becoming an author of books on Witchcraft. This put me in the public arena and allowed me to meet a wider variety of people in the Craft Community that I might not otherwise have had an opportunity to encounter. It also created a situation in which readers turned to me for direction and answers to many of their questions. In many ways this gave me greater insight into the role of the Village Witch who, long ago, provided charms, potions, protections, and counseling to the people of his or her community.

Becoming an author taught me the great responsibility of being a public Witch in a position that affects our community in many ways.

This decision to go public and write books about Witchcraft is what A Witch Like Me *is all about, individuals with the courage to stand up for what they believe in while, at the same time, giving help and guidance to those on the same path. Traditionally, this is exactly what a Witch was, a wise one with a walking storehouse of folk knowledge and a treasure trove of ancient spiritual practices.*

As in the past, being a Witch today is not always easy. Sometimes Wiccans are discriminated against because of their beliefs. Everyone who practices and writes about it knows what prejudice is. With Raven Grimassi it came in a custody fight over his daughter.

When my first marriage ended in 1972, I tried to obtain custody of my daughter. My ex-wife threatened to bring up my practice of Witchcraft in court. My attorney advised me that this would be held strongly against me in court and encouraged me to drop the case solely on this matter.

As a business-owner and member of the Downtown Business Association, the discovery of my involvement in

Witchcraft has caused a reduction in my inclusion in activities and the invitations I receive to functions. I've noticed that some people now seem to fear me in some way, and others are clearly uncomfortable in my presence. This, of course, is due to ignorance and adherence to stereotypes.

Ask the Question; The Answer is Yours

For those who practice the traditional art and craft, the connection to the Divine is the most important one. Often the Divine goes by many names, both male and female, which are all aspects of the whole. This is the beauty of the Goddess: She comes no matter what name you call her. To many Wiccans, including Raven, the Divine is the ultimate teacher. In this way, all you need to do is ask the question, and the answer will be yours.

To me, the God and Goddess are teachers, guardians, and guides. I maintain a shrine and try to honor the gods each day in one way or another. Sometimes this is through offerings and other times through song. I have a strong connection with Ceres, the Goddess of the mysteries, as I was born on her festival day.

I also have strong connections with Diana and Dianus. In my private practices, I call upon them by their older names, which are Artimite and Aplu. I believe that the gods walk with us and guide us and that we are never alone. They speak to us and to our inner spirits, and they are our companions on the Path.

The Everyday Life of Magick

Magick has been an integral part of Raven's everyday life for more than 25 years.

Magick is simply an understanding of the inner mechanisms of Nature combined with the ability to merge with and channel these forces towards a manifested desire. Affirmations of prosperity and well-being are repeated each morning while tracing a pentagram and calling upon the creative forces of Spirit over the four Elements. I join Spirit to the Elements and word my affirmations in accord with my needs for the day and the needs of others. Protections are recharged daily during the waning moon period.

I haven't experienced any healing performed on my behalf, but I have worked healing magick on others. One of the most notable experiences was the curing of a woman with a thyroid disease. Another noteworthy healing success story was freeing an individual from chronic asthma and allergies overnight. Our group does perform healing work for those who request it. Primarily, all works of magick are performed on the night of the full moon.

Raven considers the initiates in his spiritual tradition as his family.

First-degree initiation includes a form of adoption into the family. This sense of family binds us together into a relationship that is no longer "optional," any more than a blood relationship allows for options in this regard. Knowing that we are family ensures that we all work to resolve differences, stand together in adversity, and rejoice in each person's joys. Even though a person may drift off, being family means there is always a home to come back to.

Our Future

I have grave concerns about the future of Wicca. The main focus of Wicca today is upon self-styled systems, things that work for and feel right to the individual. However, it is difficult, if not impossible, to pass something useful on to another that works uniquely for oneself. This is why I believe that traditional material must be preserved, as it has stood the test of time.

Unfortunately, many modern Wiccans have a strong distaste for structure and often view it as dogmatic. Structured systems, though, tend to survive those who practice them and ensure continuation. If not for the structured systems of the past, there would have been nothing for modern eclectic systems to base their beliefs and practices upon.

As many drawn to the Wiccan path are, Raven feels a connection to the Earth, the sacred land that is the embodiment of the Goddess herself.

Anyone associated with Wicca can't help but feel the pain of the Mother Earth. We need to heal her so that she can heal us. Our connection to the Earth is our connection to the Divine.

Personally, I feel that the reason that the Earth is in such sad shape lies in the living spirit of the Earth itself. The Earth Mother is ill due to the pollution generated by modern life and due to the abuse of her resources. She thinks back to a time when the people of this planet lived in common cause with her, in harmony with her. She cries out, "Where are my children? Where are they who once honored me and walked with me? Is there no one left who will care for me as I care for them?" And so they come, people of all walks of life, hearing the call and returning to the Mother. This, I believe, is the reason for the growth of the Craft and the Goddess Movement.

7

SILVER
RAVENWOLF

I think the biggest change as far as how I view the power of the human being in concert with spirituality occurred when I used magick, ritual, and hypnotherapy to help a woman with a cancerous tumor. After six weeks of concerted effort, the tumor was gone. This made a believer out of me!

Also, when I was learning horary astrology, I cast a chart to help a family whose mother was dying of cancer. I was trying to give them assistance regarding what to do for her. Spirit must have been talking straight through me to the keyboard, because everything I wrote was accurate, and they were able to prolong her life in pleasant circumstances. She died precisely one year later—at the exact time I'd said she would a year earlier when I cast the chart. I probably could never do this again, but that certainly got me thinking about the interconnectedness with each other, ourselves, and the universe.

Silver's magickal experiences helped her write her first book, To Ride A Silver Broomstick, *in 1990. Since then, she has written more than 16 books including* To Stir A Magic Cauldron *and* Halloween! *With her books now being published in seven languages (English, German, Spanish, Danish, Portuguese, Russian and Polish) Silver has traveled across the United States and into Canada. Throughout the land, she has met thousands of others who are practicing the Craft.*

When I Knew I Was a Witch

As is the case with most individuals who are involved in the alternative religious movement, it is difficult for me to pinpoint "this was the day that I became interested." I have various childhood memories that speak of beliefs other than those of standard Christianity.

When she was 5 years old, Silver can remember sitting under a neighbor's willow tree and wishing fervently that God was a woman.

Even then, the patriarchal Sunday school did not sit well with my inner self. I thought it should be balanced, that God should have a wife. After all, my parents were married, my grandparents were partners in matrimony, and all my friends' parents were married. Why couldn't God have a partner to love? What was wrong with God, anyway? Couldn't He make a commitment? Logically, I thought, even Jesus had parents.

When she was 6 years old, Silver saw five angels at her bedroom door.

In hysterics, I told my parents. They thought that I had eaten something that did not agree with me and promptly stuffed me with medicine. Recently, when I went on tour for my angel book, I collected several real-life stories from people across the nation that made me a believer in life after death. Those who have passed on can and will assist us when we're in trouble and in daily life.

When she was 13, Silver designed a wish puppet and used him for all sorts of childhood desires, including ice cream and pretzels on a hot summer day. Around the same time a cherished, older cousin gave her a pack of tarot cards.

She told me of her idea of the universe and how it worked. It was far different than what I'd been taught in church.

At 15, Silver was accused of being a Witch by fundamentalist neighbors.

What a fuss that became, and it all began over a book that I was required to read at school entitled *The Witch and the Priest.* I happened to have it with me while visiting a friend's home. I didn't understand Fundamentalism at the time, and, although my parents attended church regularly, they weren't fanatical. Both of my parents thought my neighbors were "twisted" (the word used by my mother, as I recall) and laughed about the whole issue.

My Mother's Death

The death of Silver's mother impacted her spirituality and life in many ways.

My mother died of leukemia when I was 17. As she was dying she called everyone: Lutheran and Baptist ministers, a Jewish rabbi, and a Catholic priest. She said she didn't care what they were, as long as they prayed like the dickens for her. The standard Christian religions did not support her or my father during her terminal illness, nor did they make any effort to help my family. Many wanted to take our money or simply "save the family from future hellish prospects," in the ministers' words.

Silver's mother had been a kind woman. Her horrible death and the treatment by supposed holy people created a permanent alteration in Silver's attitude toward God, religion, and spirituality.

I went searching for something better than what I had. I found my answers in the alternative religion of Wicca. The faith was simple, free of burgeoning dogma, celebrated the Divine in the female as well as the male, and seemed to me to be a positive, proactive way to work with spirituality.

Although Silver had many magickal experiences as a child, the first serious ritual she ever performed was during the time when her mother was dying and in great pain.

At the time I had no official training. However, I felt that my circumstances demanded I do something. I had nowhere to turn, so I wrote the ritual myself and performed it in my bedroom. Basically, I begged Spirit to take me in place of my mother or, if that was not possible, to give her a quick and easy passing. She died less than six hours later—after weeks of languishing in a hospital bed.

When she did that first ritual for her mother, Silver also promised that she would help people when she could rather than looking the other way.

I've tried my best to fulfill that oath. I realize now that you don't have to beg, that Spirit has more respect for us than that. But I came from a Christian background, and it was the only thing I knew to do at the time.

Deeper into Wicca

Now that Wicca has been a part of Silver's life for more than 27 years, she admits it is difficult for her to think about what life would be like without it.

In my early days of learning, I had an abusive husband (not the man I am married to now). I worked two jobs. With Wicca and its spirituality, I was able to work my way out of that mess and still retain my sanity, but it was a long process, because I had to change in order for my life to change. As I moved deeper into Witchcraft, I would look around at people outside of my faith and think how about horrid it would be to not have magick in my life. Life would be so dull.

I think that Wicca offers the seeker a no-money-down, no-expected-payment type of religious environment that many individuals find appealing. It concentrates on changing the you within, rather than expecting you to pull more members into the fold to support your sense of validation. The Divine Feminine is also extremely appealing, as well as its proactive support, which encourages you to reach for your goals and to mold your life into what you feel is the ultimate.

The Goddess and Spirit

Silver speaks of her relationship with the Goddess as a one-on-one affair.

I talk to Deity all the time and implement spirituality as much as possible in my daily life. Although I work with all sorts of spiritual energy, I am a Priestess of the Morrighan.

Silver RavenWolf and her husband of 20 years, Mick, both involve themselves in the study of Wicca, including conducting studies in their home in Pennsylvania. Her group practices Euro-Wicca, a mixture of Witchcraft and

German and American Folk Magick called the Black Forest Clan and Seminary. Currently, there are 22 covens in 18 states, as well as one in Canada. These covens do not hive; they stay a part of the overall organization. Training involves four years or more of dedicated work on the part of the student and supports family unity and participation.

Unlike many groups, our students have become adept in assisting people in some of the tougher areas of human relations. We often practice magick and ritual to help the authorities capture criminals, though this is by no means the extent of our work.

Because my training has also consisted of work in the folk magick arena, I have learned to work with deities of various paths.

We also do a lot of healing work for all sorts of medical and psychological issues. In all honesty, we've had so many successful workings I don't know where to begin. In our group we call it "trying" (*besprecken,* after the Pennsylvania Dutch word), which doesn't attribute the success to us, but rather to Spirit.

We've also had success with what I call "stealth" maladies, where the doctors have no clue what's wrong. Spirit always knows, even if the physicians don't.

Wicca and Family

I have four children who range in age from 15 to 21. Due to family responsibilities, my husband and I limit our speaking engagements, depending on events at home. For example, last year Falcon graduated from high school, and we wanted to be home for the prom and graduation. I realized early in my career that I would have to make compromises involving public engagements so that my children didn't feel that my career was taking away from our home life.

Silver has made a focused effort not only to expose her children to the Wiccan path, but also to familiarize them with the various religions available in her area. They visited a Jewish synagogue, attended a Catholic Mass every Christmas Eve, and participated in a Baptist church camp over the summer. They talked to Mormons, visited a Seventh Day Adventist revival, and experienced a Native American Indian celebration.

I did not accompany them on these various jaunts; I preferred to send them with individuals of those faiths, people who could answer their questions without my interference.

When they returned home, we discussed what they liked, what they didn't like, and how they felt about each segment of religious belief. They had the opportunity to see the community and mechanics of other religions, and they are better prepared to deal with the difficult socialization process of the teen years.

Silver's family, including her Lutheran father, is deeply involved in the Black Forest Clan and her career. On occasion, her children speak in public, give interviews, assist in answering fan mail, and make helpful suggestions on what to include in her books and training materials.

My husband and I travel and minister together as a team. My father has always been helpful in governmental decisions made for our Clan. Recently, he has been attending my book signings with his camera so that we can document some of our work.

My entire family knows that I am a practicing Witch and Wiccan author. Everybody knows. Arguments within a family environment over Wicca usually aren't about religion at all.

They either stem from inner-dynamic control issues far older than the new religious choice or from the detractor's fear that his or her religious validation is being threatened. Both issues belong to the individual who does not like Wicca, not to the individual in the family who wishes to practice it.

With that in mind, we've never had a problem, because we've told them bluntly that if they don't like it, it's their problem. They can deal with it on their own terms. As we took this position in the beginning of our spiritual growth, we've never had a problem.

In their travels, Silver has focused on the seminars, book signings, and the spiritual aspects of the Craft and Paganism, and Mick has concentrated on learning Craft hierarchy, government, and the intricacies of the group mind.

He spent many late evenings talking to Craft elders around the country, learning what we need as a community, how to create positive change, and how to govern ourselves in a spiritual, non-restrictive way.

None of these topics has an easy answer. As our own Black Forest Clan grew, my husband and I realized that to meet the needs of my readers and our religious organization, we needed to keep an open mind and non-biased attitude. Therefore, I am a Witch and my husband is a Pagan. He prefers that his lineage be separate from mine.

Silver feels that her belief system has strengthened her marriage and helped her to be a better parent.

I constantly consider the feelings of my husband and my children. We have a harmonious family environment, and I'm very proud of that, considering today's difficult times. Our family observes the holidays and coven functions together, though at times we do separate rituals depending upon our schedules.

Practicing Magick Every Day

My writing in itself is magick, and I write about 4,000 words a day on various topics, not all of which enters the standard publishing market. I write training material for the Black Forest Clan and answer letters from fans and community members who need research assistance or who are in trouble. I practice daily and seasonal devotions. I also travel around the country a great deal, giving lectures and doing signings and seminars. There is also the administration of the Black Forest Clan, which often requires spiritual decisions, spiritual work, and attending group ritual on a cyclical basis.

The members of the Black Forest Clan come from nearly all walks of life, including teachers, medical professionals, students, blue-collar workers, college professors, law enforcement officers, writers, actors, and business owners. They are spread across the United States and Canada as a huge extended family.

We designed Black Forest to function that way. Spouses and partners, although they may not be Wiccan, are also considered a part of our family and are treated equally. Having so many people tied together over long distances gives them all a sense of empowerment. When the chips are down you can always call, e-mail, or visit a brother or sister and find the support that you need.

Because of her high profile as a Witch, Silver has faced discrimination in the past, especially in various jobs.

At one job, I was told, "We don't want your kind here." I was fired from another job, although I couldn't prove it was based on my interest in Wicca.

My children have experienced subtle forms of discrimination through the school system and from other children whose families are new to the area. We've also had distinct difficulties with teachers, though most of this has stemmed from their personalities rather than religious dogma. This has been a major contention in our lives and will continue to be so until our last child is out of school. We homeschooled one of our children for a short time due to our distaste of the current educational process.

Nevertheless, it is exciting to watch a new form of faith evolve and grow and to frankly realize that this faith will have labor pains. If Witchcraft continues to meet the needs of people in a positive way, then it will grow.

RAYMOND BUCKLAND

Considered one of the leading authorities on Voodoo, Witchcraft, and the supernatural, Raymond Buckland has spent nearly half a century investigating the occult and has been practicing Wicca for more than 25 years. Initiated by Gerald Gardner's High Priestess, Lady Olwen, in 1963, he has practiced magick considerably longer than most in the current Wicca movement.

No one simply knows when they are a Witch, in that no one is a Witch until they are *made* one through initiation or a self-dedication. You cannot be born a Witch any more than you can be born a Roman Catholic. You can be born into a Witch family, but you do not actually become a Witch yourself until you are initiated.

A Fascination with the Occult

Since my teens, I have been interested in all occult matters. I first read my uncle's books on spiritualism when I was about 12 years old. My interest and reading about the occult eventually led me to the works of Margaret Murray and Gerald Gardner. After reading these books, I realized that Witchcraft was the religion I had been looking for, even though I had not consciously been looking. I wrote to Gardner and went on from there.

Ray Buckland first came to the United States from England in 1962, where he wrote television comedy scripts for British television. Since then, he has gone on to publish more than 30 books on Witchcraft and the supernatural, with more than one million copies collectively in print. In addition, he has appeared on several talk shows, including The Dick Cavett Show *and* Tom Snyder's Tomorrow Show. *Ray has certainly been one the most visible Witches within the public arena.*

A Magickal Initiation

His first conscious magickal experience happened during his first time in the Circle: at his initiation in 1963.

I think most people would say that their initiation was the most intense experience of their lives. I know mine was. It is something that will live with me for the rest of my life. I had been looking forward to my initiation for a long time, and, as the time drew near, I got more and more nervous and excited. Part of the reason was knowing that it was not life-threatening, yet there was the fear of the unknown; I had no idea what I might be put through. I kept telling myself that if Lady Olwen—a petite lady—could go through it, then so could I! Exact details are, of course, secret. It was a fairly lengthy ritual, but I seemed to float through it, accepting everything and absorbing the beauty of the rite.

At the Drawing Down the Moon ritual, where the Goddess herself descends into the High Priestess, I saw a striking physical change take place with my High Priestess, Lady Olwen. She changed completely. She was normally a woman of about 40, with the little lines and "crow's feet" on the face that go with that age. Yet when the Goddess descended into her, her face changed completely. All the lines disappeared, and she looked as if she were about 18 years old. I have not seen such a dramatic change since.

Wicca in the 1960s

Having been initiated and begun practicing Witchcraft in the freewheeling 1960s, Ray found both a tolerance and a prejudice towards his spiritual choice. On one hand, there was an openness and a tolerance towards people and ideas in general, as evidenced in the "different strokes for different folks" 1960s saying.

I was generally well-accepted into the community, mainly because my neighbors knew me and my family before they got to know what our religious preference was.

On the other hand, there was a world that was trying to rattle his windows and break down his walls.

In what I call the "early days" in the 1960s, it was not easy. I suffered a lot, as did my family. I had my car set on fire, bricks thrown through my window, and my door kicked in, and I received a certain amount of general verbal and physical harassment. Happily, I was always on very good terms with the local police.

Not only did Raymond Buckland persevere and make it through the experience of being harassed for what he believed in, but he continued to write books and give workshops on Witchcraft. As is the case with many people practicing modern Wicca, Ray's personal spiritual practices have evolved into something that works for him.

Becoming a Solitary Practitioner

Today I practice a mixture of Saxon, Scottish, and whatever feels right. I was, for many years, Gardnerian, and then I founded the Seax-Wica tradition. I was involved with covens for about 25 years or so, before becoming a solitary practitioner (which I am now).

After practicing a spiritual tradition for a long while, many individuals, including Ray, become "solitary practitioners," choosing to practice their spirituality without a group. Sometimes solitary practitioners practice Wicca with their immediate families, with a partner, or solo. Ultimately, it is a person's connection to the Divine that is important. Everything else is irrelevant. Whether you choose to practice your spirituality and connection to the Divine by yourself or in a group is totally up to you. That is part of the beauty of Wicca: The choice is yours.

Ray's Romani Roots and Family

For many people, Wicca leads them to a connection with their genetic roots, whether they be Celtic, Greek, or Native American. With Raymond Buckland, Wicca has helped him to become connected to his Romani ancestry.

Ray's grandfather was the first of the Buckland gypsies to give up traveling the roads in wagons and to settle in a permanent house. From his earliest childhood memories, Ray recalls watching his grandmother tell fortunes and read the cards.

Nowadays Ray uses Romani deities exclusively in his magickal works. He has even gone so far as to adapt a healing technique to the Romani tradition.

I was singled out as a healer in my earliest days in the Craft and have done healing ever since. I used to do individual healing and coven healing. Recently, I have developed a Romani form that I find to be extremely effective, and I do this healing technique whenever the need arises.

My mother knew about my involvement with the Craft and was very interested. She died at the age of 101. My father, unfortunately, died before I came into the Craft, but I think he would have been very interested. I have two sons by my first wife. We had family circles when they were both young. My elder son was initiated when he was 7. My younger son never had any interest, so he was not initiated. Today they are both in their 40s. My elder son seldom practices; my younger one is now more interested, but not to the point of coming in.

Life as a Wiccan Author

With the publications of his first books on Witchcraft, such as Witchcraft…The Religion *and* Witchcraft Ancient and Modern, *Raymond Buckland became one of the first Witches who was willing to write down his experiences, reaching out to others who were having the same experiences. Male-dominated Christian beliefs did not fill the void, and people were searching for something more, a path to the Divine where everything connects.*

Oneness is the path where the Goddess and God are One, which is what Deity is all about: not one or the other, but all.

Ray feels that the most empowering aspects of Wicca are the knowledge that you are a part of Nature, not apart from it.

You have the God and the Goddess with you at all times. I think we all practice magick every day, in one form or another. I don't do ritual every day or even every month. I do it if it is called for. Otherwise, it is more a form of Hedge Witchcraft that I practice magickally.

Hedge Witchcraft is like "folk Craft" in that it follows a path set down by the local healers, midwives, and seers of the past. In the same way as a traditional Shaman, a good Hedge Witch has a solid knowledge of locally grown herbs and their medicinal and culinary uses. Hedge Witches are usually solitary Witches who, so to speak, "do their own thing."

Starting a Coven in the United States

My initiation was obviously my most magickal experience, but the second would have to be the process of starting a coven and establishing the Craft here in the United States, as well as the responsibility that goes with it.

Ray has always considered his coven his extended family.

It empowers me as much as any family group. We are empowered by being close. Wicca is a constant, life-changing experience!

In many ways it was not easy getting the Craft started in the United States. As Gardner's books began to circulate, more and more people decided that they wanted to be part of the

Old Religion. Anyone writing to Gerald would have his or her letter forwarded to me. I was the "clearinghouse" here in the United States. At that time, we were taught to be cautious and to take time in examining those who wanted to come in, making quite sure that they were right for the Craft and that the Craft was right for them. There was a strict year-and-a-day waiting period before initiation and also between each of the degrees.

We (my High Priestess, the Lady Rowen, and I) stuck to our teachings. We were criticized for it as being aloof and snobbish. People had discovered Wicca and they wanted in! We did grow gradually, expanding with and having other covens break off from ours over the years. But there were many who refused to wait—and were "inspired" by such books and movies as *Rosemary's Baby*—who took it upon themselves to start their own spurious "covens" based on what little knowledge they had gathered and making up the rest.

Happily, we were able to give the true Craft a good solid foundation in this country. It was frustrating to not be able to bring everyone in right away, but if we had done that, there would have been no control over who was truly dedicated and who was trying to get in just for what they thought to be sex, drugs, and titillating magick.

At that time, too, our names and address got out and we went through the same persecution that Gerald had gone through when he first came out into the open. I had dedicated my life to straightening the image of the Craft, though, so we endured it.

Despite the criticism we had to endure, I would not change the way we did things. Later we were joined by others, such as Sybil Leek, and the Craft gradually started to grow in the right direction.

A Mover and a Shaker

I don't think there are any comparisons between my life prior to Wicca and since. It gave me a direction in life and, and most important to me, helped me develop my writing and teaching skills so that I could bring Wicca to others. I really couldn't imagine life without Wicca now.

Because Wicca is a religion with autonomous covens and no one leader of it all, there will never be the same front presented that is found with most other established religions. But anything that helps us be accepted as "just another religion" can only be a help to stop the misconceptions. The more people discover what Witchcraft actually is, the more they will embrace it. However, we should never proselytize, merely educate.

I have been a mover and a shaker, having spent the first 30 years or so of my Wiccan life writing, lecturing, teaching, and establishing the Craft in this country. I feel I have done my share and am much less active these days, although I still write as much, if not more, than ever. There are others who carry the torch and, with all that we have discussed, I feel there is a very positive path ahead for Witchcraft.

Lady Sabrina

The major draw of Wicca is the magick, particularly the magick of achieving your goals. You can go to any church and pray to the Divine. They all have special times and celebrations, whether it's Christmas or Hanukkah. The fundamental aspects of Wicca are the same: We worship God, celebrate the times of power, get together for social occasions, and, pray for those things we want.

When people find magick, they realize that they have the power to do something for themselves, independent of an outside force. I also think people like the idea of personal responsibility. I like the idea that I am responsible for my goals and achievements so that I can revel in them.

In most Christian religions, if you do something good, then God is responsible for it. If you do something bad, then the devil is responsible for it. You are basically a nonentity—not responsible for your actions, good or bad.

In Wicca, you are responsible for everything you do, and I think people like that. They like the fact they can do a love spell or a spell for a job promotion. You can make your choices. You are responsible for your actions, and you have the ability to make changes in your life. Most religions other than Wicca don't offer this.

I hate people who say you shouldn't use magick to manipulate the forces. If you do a healing, you are manipulating the forces. If you want to do a love spell to attract a particular person to fall in love with you, then go ahead and do it. But when Tuesday morning rolls around and you decide you don't like the color of his socks, you can't say, "Be gone foul thing" and kick him out of your life. It doesn't work that way. There's no difference between doing a candle spell and using courting tools in the form of a short skirt and perfume.

Creating Our Lady of Enchantment

No stranger to magick and Wicca, Lady Sabrina has been teaching Witchcraft for more than 20 years. As High Priestess and founder of the Our Lady of Enchantment seminary of Wicca, she holds Friday night churches and conducts classes that get people involved in doing magick. How involved? She has taught more than 25,000 students!

We have seven home-study courses as well as a religious arts program for those who wish to get legal "Wiccan" ministerial credentials. Our most popular courses are Earth, Religion, & Power (the basic Wicca course), Metaphysics I, and Spell Crafting. These three courses also make up the majority of our Religious Arts and Science Degree.

It was 23 years ago, in September 1978, that I started Our Lady of Enchantment. At that time, there was very little available on Wicca as a religion, and only a few groups and organizations that were oriented toward teaching. At the time I lived in California, and for the most part, the public end of the Craft consisted of folks trying to preserve (or immortalize) the dying hippie movement. At the other end of the spectrum were the "ceremonial magicians," whose long-involved and sometimes complex rites would tax even the most patient of devotees. Basically your choices were pretty limited.

So with some encouragement from others of like mind, I started the school and our first course (Earth, Religion, & Power) based on what I had been taught before, during, and after initiation. The course provided basic information that anyone, regardless of his or her level of training or development, could use to build his or her own spiritual system from.

When you think about it, a Wicca school is a gift, especially if it offers home-study courses. If it were possible to learn all you needed to know from books, we would have no schools; we'd need only libraries. Our Lady of Enchantment offers the student a safe, structured program, real teachers, and, for those who live in the New England area, a place to celebrate the beauty and power of the Wiccan religion.

Lady Sabrina has also written several books on Witchcraft, including Exploring Wicca *and* The Witch's Master Grimoire. *Making no secret of her spirituality, she talks candidly and openly about being a modern-day Witch. Her classes, books, and public appearances demonstrate her courage to stand up for her beliefs and to be part of the blossoming movement of Wicca.*

I Always Liked Religion

I was raised Catholic. I always wanted to go to church, because I liked religion from day one. When I was 5 years old,

I sat in my room, where I had a little altar that had a statue of Mother Mary on it. I had an older lady, a babysitter, who practically raised me. She was always helping me put things on the altar. If it was Fall, we would get leaves and acorns. For some odd reason, my mother allowed me to have little sticks of incense. She didn't like me playing with fire, but there was nothing she could do about it.

One early magickal experience that Lady Sabrina remembers occurred as she was walking up the staircase as a child.

It was in a big house. At the top of the stairs was a window, and in the window I saw the face of the Green Man. Only being 6 at the time, I thought it was the devil, of course. After all, I was Catholic and attended an all-girls Catholic academy. Years later, when I became involved in the Craft, I found out who it was.

I became interested in the Craft when I was 27 years old. I was an avid mystery reader—Agatha Christie, Phyllis Whitney, pretty much anybody. Barbara Michaels was my favorite. I was looking for a book in the mystery section of a bookstore in the 1970s, and there, in the middle of the section, was a book called *The Witches' Workbook* by Anne Grammery.

After reading the book, everything clicked, and I suddenly felt like I had the world in my hands.

Inside the book was a coupon for an occult book club. I filled out the card, and a week later when I came home, there was a box of books sitting on my doorstep. I opened the box and found 10 books and a deck of tarot cards. The odd thing is, I never received a bill for them.

Later on, I was in the checkout line at the grocery store, thumbing through one of the tabloids. I found Gavin Bone's ad and sent away for information. From this I started his course.

Along with his own books, he had other books listed, so I started reading a variety of sources, such as *What Witches Do* by Farrar. I took about four lessons of Gavin's course and decided I wanted to be initiated.

My Initiation

Lady Sabrina lived in California at the time, so Gavin put her in contact with someone in Arizona, which had the closest coven to her.

I felt I had to go to Arizona, which is why I am so fanatical about the initiation process. I don't believe in self-initiation. You can't take yourself through the threshold and test yourself the same way someone else would.

Lady Sabrina calls her initiation a little odd, because the only training she had were the courses she had taken from Gavin. These were all from a fairly patriarchal point of view.

Gavin didn't stress feminine tools such as the chalice. I had made some of my tools. When I arrived in Arizona, Bob and Dorothy, the High Priest and High Priestess, looked at these things and asked, "What the hell is that?" I said, "That's my ankh." Bob said, "It looks like a rug beater." Then he asked, "Where's your chalice?" to which I replied, "What's a chalice?" The whole thing was a virginal experience for me.

When I arrived, Dorothy was in a snit because she and Bob had had a fight. She refused to meet or initiate me. She was absolutely not going to do it. So I said to Bob, "Give me five minutes in the other room," because I was really good with magick. I went in and did my thing with a candle. I had never met the woman. About a half hour later, Dorothy agreed to at least meet me, which was the least she could do. We met, but she told me that she just couldn't do the initiation because she and Bob weren't getting along. Bob and I went to lunch and when we returned, I told him, "She'll agree to do it." About 45 minutes later, she agreed to do it. Bob said, "I don't know what you were doing in the room, but don't you ever do it to me."

Because of her reading, Lady Sabrina could do candle magick, but she didn't know anything about Wicca.

Dorothy, the High Priestess came, and she and Bob initiated me on the full moon on the Summer Solstice. When I returned home, it was really odd. Have you ever seen a movie called *The Invasion of the Body Snatchers*? Well, that's sort of how everyone treated me. They looked at me and said, "We know that's Cathy, but what the heck did they do to her? She looks the same, but there's something so different about her." I was different from that moment on.

Lady Sabrina admits that she doesn't know what happened in the circle the night of her initiation. What she does remember was throwing up all over everyone.

I didn't have anything in my stomach but water. As I was brought, blindfolded and tied up, into the circle, I heard these big doors open and then shut. I felt walls of flames going up around me. I don't remember anything else until after the ritual, when we were all sitting around eating. People kept saying that I was glowing.

Working with the Goddess and God

The divine energy I work with mostly is the Greek goddess Hecate. I have a statue of her. I've tried other deities, but I always come back to her. For me, there's something special about Hecate.

When she holds her Friday night church meetings, which are open to the public, Lady Sabrina uses Kerridwen and Kernunnos almost 100 percent of the time.

We've been doing Friday night church for more than 20 years now. Using Kerridwen and Kernunnos makes things easier because all of the rituals are written out, and using the same deities all the time simplifies things because you aren't trying to substitute one goddess for another. That can be confusing.

The other reason for using the same goddess and god each time we do rituals is that it builds up and establishes an energy bank that can be built upon. People who have never been to anything like our seminary walk into the chapel and gasp because of the immense amount of energy they feel. They don't realize that it's been building for 20 years, creating a vortex of energy.

Friday night church with Lady Sabrina is indeed an extraordinary spiritual experience.

We have five works that we do: meditation, prayer chest, crystal charging, candle blessing, and the talisman. The idea is to build both skill level and Sabbat energy.

We begin our cycle in December. That is when each person projects for long-term goals, such as a job promotion. We do works on each of the Sabbats to enhance that intended goal. In meditation, the members formulate it and think about it, and then the next time they come to church we have the prayer chest, where everybody writes out their wishes or desires. Those wishes are put into the chest, then blessed and charged in the circle.

The next time church members attend service, they bring their crystal with them. It represents what they want, such as their boss noticing them more for that job promotion, so maybe they bring citrine and charge it with this energy. Next is a candle blessing, where members bring an orange or yellow candle for attraction or whatever they're working on. Everybody is different. They work on their goals at home. Bringing their goals to circle gives them an extra charge of energy. The last one is talisman, where members put together a talisman for the same goal. Not only do they have the eight Pagan Sabbats to work through, but they also have the Friday night churches. Things are simple with one focus, depending on whether it's the meditation or whatever.

How and Why I Started Writing

I had already started the school when someone suggested I write the Wicca course. I was a member of COG (Covenant of the Goddess), and they didn't like Gavin's stuff because it was male-oriented. So when I finished the course, I ran an ad for a Wicca course and started getting sign-ups. When it came time for the COG meeting, I took my ill-gotten gains and showed them off for everybody. They all accused me of selling the Craft and wouldn't speak to me.

Why does anyone write a book? To express their inner thoughts on a subject in a manner that can be shared with others of like mind. With my seventh book in the works for New Page Books, I think the main reason that I do what I do is for the school. The books provide additional information for our students and reinforce the positive and accessible side of the Craft as we practice it at Our Lady of Enchantment.

Of course if you want total honesty, most of us write books for the credibility, the admiration from our peers, and, hopefully, the money they will bring us.

As far as how books have changed my life, probably the most significant factor is that they have given the school, and our teachings, more credibility. They have helped to build confidence in our teachings. After all, if a book publisher sees fit to publish your ideas, they must be worth looking into!

Everything Has its Time

As many other Wiccan authors do, Lady Sabrina sees Wicca becoming popular because it's the right time.

Everything has its time. There was a reason for Christianity. It pulled things out of the mud, muck, and mire and gave splendor, majesty, and organization to spirituality. It reached its peak, and now it's time for something else to come in.

People are tired of being ushered in and out of buildings the way cattle are. They are tired of being told what to think, what to do, how to feel, and that they're not allowed to get involved. When we do ritual, we involve as many people as we can, and we switch off with the priesthood. I don't act as High Priestess every time. When I was initiated, Dorothy did everything, but we don't do it that way. We switch off. The initiates are the ones who do the rite of union, casting the circle, and calling in the guardians. There are a lot of other parts that people can do.

I imagine at some point, whether Wiccans choose to believe it or not, Wicca will be organized and structured and that there will be Wiccan churches everywhere. It will be as accepted the way Christianity is today. I don't think it can be avoided, and I don't think it *should* be avoided. Christianity was around for 500 years before it took off. It started with people meeting in small groups in their homes. It was the same thing. Wicca is just in its beginning stages.

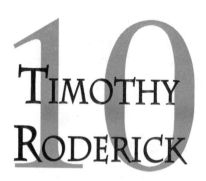

TIMOTHY
RODERICK

I think most Witches, myself included, know from an early age that there is something "different" or magickal about our lives. As far back as I can remember, I was always playing at being a magickal person. I felt as though I was casting spells and seeing spirits.

Timothy Roderick had many magickal experiences in the natural setting of Lyme Kiln Canyon, near his childhood home in the north end of the San Fernando Valley.

I remember making spirit dolls from the long grasses of the canyon and having mystical encounters with the local wildlife. Witchcraft is a path that calls you to it from an early age. I'm certain that most readers can think back on their own lives and recall their own childhood magickal experiences that were precursors to finding their way to Wicca.

Tim's path to Wicca has led him to write books such as Apprentice to Power *and* Dark Moon Mysteries. *He explores subjects such as animal familiars and the Jungian "shadow self," and, by doing so, he touches upon both the bright and dark aspects of the Goddess and God, within and without.*

A Good Candidate for the Priesthood

When I was a child, I would look out of my upstairs bedroom window and see the tops of nearby trees. I found that if I concentrated enough on the trees, the leaves would move a little. Before long, a wind would begin to blow, and the leaves would dance madly. I experienced my connection with the wind and the trees as a powerful magickal bond.

To tell you the truth, I am surprised at where I am today, when I think in terms of the spiritual path I've followed throughout the course of my life. I grew up Catholic, and my parents thought I was a good candidate for the priesthood around the time that I made the transition to high school. I went to a Catholic school for my elementary school years, and my eighth-grade graduating class voted me "most likely to become a priest." (Of course, from one 12-year-old to another, that was supposed to be an insult.) I wasn't sure what to think of it, but it certainly did wake me up to the fact that other people thought of me in a spiritual way.

As far back as Tim can remember, he was always doing things such as casting spells, trying to predict the future, and seeing spirits.

I think I frightened my parents on more than one occasion when told them things about the spirits that I "saw" living in our house.

By the time Tim began college, he had serious doubts about Catholicism. That was when he began to earnestly explore alternative spiritual paths.

The paths that spoke to me the most were earth religions, Shamanism and Wicca. When I was 18 years old, I decided to take a class at a local bookstore that was notorious for being owned by Witches. *Who were these Witches, anyway?* I wondered. I had already ventured outside of my religious upbringing by questioning and searching, so I felt I had nothing to lose by taking an introductory class in Wicca. That was when the whole world opened up to me—when I really understood the value of stepping outside of the little zones of safety we human beings like to set up for ourselves.

My Journey into Wicca

Once he was introduced to real Witches, Tim began his journey of training as well as authentic, self-motivated spiritual exploration.

Over time, my spiritual understanding, as all things do, evolved. So did my approach to the Craft. As I look back at my own writings, I can see the chronicles of my own spiritual progression.

I trained with a circle of Gardnerian Witches in Los Angeles for several years. Then I studied magickal practice with a woman who was a Shaman in a Native American tradition. The combination of Wicca and Shamanic practice helped me to see a correlation between the two systems. That was when I decided to write my book, *The Once Unknown Familiar.*

The Birth of the EarthDance Collective

It was around that same time that I decided to start my own Gardnerian coven in the Los Angeles area. That was the beginning of EarthDance Collective, which is a southern California–based collective of individuals who are interested in the creative-collaborative exploration of Wicca. The name "EarthDance" applies a Shamanic approach to traditional Witchcraft practices. Drumming, dancing, ecstatic practices, and other mystical means of spiritual exploration guide us toward sudden awakenings and magickal openings of power.

Our spiritual work focuses on realizing the mythic, archetypal, and spiritual dimensions of the ancient magickal customs of Old Europe. We strive to embody the essence of these customs in our daily lives, and we endeavor to recognize the Sacred in all. EarthDance emphasizes the individual cultivation of wisdom and insight as a means to mystical, personal empowerment.

Through our practices, we provide a unique approach to Wicca that is grounded in practical matters and that aids participants in finding Goddess and God in everyday life. Collectively, our spiritual work includes Pagan seasonal observances, insight training, divination, ecstatic drumming and dancing, and other forms of deeply transformative magickal work.

Since 1992, we have sponsored community-wide rituals, workshops, and spiritual retreats. Our training in Wicca focuses on learning through two distinct paths. One path focuses on learning techniques and basic information through conventional, linear means, and the other path emphasizes an intuitive, mystic understanding.

The members of EarthDance Collective are wonderful people. In a way, we do form our own family. Each member takes on a role and provides some form of healing or nurturing to other members. In that sense, we are akin to a "functional" family.

At the same time, we all respect boundaries and understand that each of us is on this life journey to learn and to understand who and what we are. We also know that the process of unveiling the mysteries of our being is one that can require space and understanding. So we offer each other support in a way that allows for individual growth.

Arriving at my True Spiritual Home

Tim's first ritual experience involving Wicca had a profound impact on his spirituality.

When I was 19 years old, I was invited to an open Beltane ritual in Long Beach, California. I can still envision that event clearly. There must have been 50 people attending this circle. I had never seen anything like it before. Here were folks gathered together in the names of the Old Ones.

For some reason, up until that point in my magickal practice, I assumed that there weren't many people involved in the Craft. But I was wrong. It dawned on me that there must have been hundreds, if not thousands, of ritual circles going on throughout the world on that Beltane day.

The ritual itself was simple. Each of us offered a bundle of twigs to a central fire. When my turn came to make the offering, I recall this warm, tingling feeling that came over me.

It was then that I knew that I had arrived at my true spiritual home with Wicca.

One later experience also factored in heavily in Tim's spiritual progression, an experience that he talks about in his book, Apprentice to Power.

When I was 28 years old, I was kidnapped and held hostage at gunpoint. I was as close to being violently murdered as anyone can come.

As you might imagine, it was a horrendously frightening ordeal that yielded both desirable and undesirable results. After the event, I went numb for an entire year. I was fearful and angry and sad. I wondered, *How could this have happened to me?* I felt as though my spiritual practice was strong and that I was magickally protected, yet I came face to face with my own mortality. I didn't know what to do with the experience.

The experience caused me to completely reevaluate my approach to my spiritual practices. I had to really grope around in the darkness of my own fears and insecurities, because at that time there were no formal Wiccan practices that could address such powerful stuff.

It was out of Tim's spiritual explorations around darkness that his book Dark Moon Mysteries *emerged.*

Dark Moon Mysteries is all about working with the darker aspects of magickal energy. We are all made up of both dark and light energy, as expressed in the familiar Asian yin-yang symbol. In Western cultures in particular, we tend to look away, discount, and even separate ourselves from anything that may seem dark. But the dark is part of who we are, what the Earth is, and what life is when you consider it as a whole.

Darkness occurs on the personal realm as "shadow." Shadows represent the forbidden, dangerous, or unthinkable aspects that we all carry within. They can be our anger, rage, sadness, grief, selfishness, cruelty, aggression, and so forth. My book is filled with insights, rituals, meditations, and exercises to help magickal folk recognize their darker aspects and incorporate them into their lives in a way that promotes healing and magickal empowerment.

My Current Wiccan Practices

I mostly practice a Shamanic form of Wicca. A Shamanic approach is both the theological and practical background of EarthDance Collective as well.

Over the years of my spiritual practice in Wicca, I have found that the Craft I practice has very little to do with beliefs. It has more to do with experience. I would say that my foundational beliefs are really foundational experiences. I experience the world as an expression of the Divine. I experience myself as divine as well.

Tim has come to realize that each second in time is precious.

Every moment is a moment of divinity. That means that each activity I do, each breath that I take, each word I speak holds power. My task in each moment is to constantly see into that power and that divinity. My personal rituals and the rituals and celebrations of EarthDance Collective all evolve from this immediate experience of Nature and divinity.

Not many people take the time to consider their relationship with Deity, but it is this relationship that defines how an individual will live his or her life. I find that my relationship with Deity is one that pervades every moment of my existence. The gods can't be partitioned or categorized. They can't be placed in little boxes and wrapped up after a magick circle.

Deity in the World Is Fact

The concept of Deity in the world is not just a nice idea; it is fact. It takes a long time and a lot of mystical work to finally penetrate our own barriers enough to discover the truth. But once you arrive, you discover that Deity is right here, right now. Whatever you're doing in this moment is an aspect of Deity. Your breath, body, thoughts, feelings, and actions all come from the Divine.

I've always felt that myth and symbol pervade Wicca in a meaningful way. The gods and goddesses are archetypes, symbols of the energies and experiences of our own lives. Instead of calling on a god or goddess, I look to see what theme seems to be coming up in my life. Then I match that up with one of the god or goddess energies.

My public Craft name is Dionus, which is a stylization of the Greek Dionysus. When I came to that magickal name, I found that it was a good representation of a major theme in my spiritual explorations. Dionysus is also called "the Twice Born"; he was a child of humanity and one of the Divine. I found that it was a good name to symbolize my ongoing quest for spiritual renewal. It helped me to remember my place in the grand scheme of things. So for me, the gods and goddesses are a way of recognizing the spiritual Nature of my life no matter what the circumstance.

Magick as a Transformational Process

Dion Fortune is often quoted as the one who said that magick is the "ability to change consciousness" at will. I've always been drawn to the idea of magick being a transformational process. If you examine the processes of magick very carefully, you'll discover that magick is a matter of changing your mind about your relationship to things and people in the world.

But from what to what are we supposed to change our consciousness? That's a question that, when contemplated, can lead to some real insight. I believe that magick is changing consciousness from a perspective of disunity to one of unity. In other words, it is a process of removing the blocks between the magician and the thing desired. It is a difficult thing to do, but that is the primary work of any mystic.

It seems to me that if magick is about changing consciousness, then magick is something I work on daily. One of the ways that I practice magick is through daily meditations. I clear my mind so that I can see more plainly the baseline of reality: that the rest of the world and I are interdependent and wonderfully woven together.

Tim feels that Wicca offers something that other Western religious systems do not.

Wicca offers a direct pathway to discovering our true nature. That's no small feat. Through this pathway, we find our own link to the Divine. Wicca also allows us to practice our spiritual path at own pace. It allows a great deal of freedom in the methods that we use to explore our spiritual path. For these reasons, I find Wicca an empowering path.

I think that anyone who contributes to the expansion of knowledge in the Craft moves and shakes the paradigm. With each new book comes a new perspective; something new is then dredged up from the collective unconscious. It is this material from our collective experiences and research that will always shape our spiritual path.

The Challenge We Face

Tim doesn't talk about his spiritual path within his community unless he is specifically asked to do so.

Being a Witch changes everything, including how others relate to you. I think any time one explores an alternative spiritual path the usual community reaction is one of disdain.

Tim has experienced some discrimination because of his spirituality, particularly in his professional career.

One incident comes to mind in which I felt forced to end a job because of my Wiccan visibility. A zealous Christian co-worker had seen my face on the cover of my book *Dark Moon Mysteries,* and she decided that she could not "suffer a Witch" to work in peace. My job involved dealings with foster families and foster children. This co-worker decided to inform the families with whom I worked that they were dealing with a Witch.

Needless to say, families began calling the company and lodging complaints about a "Satanist" working with their children. Although the firm was supportive of me, I realized that it would be difficult to repair the damage that was already done, so I moved on. (The company fired that Christian co-worker before I left.)

What I have found interesting is that, although my family members are Catholic, no one has ever tried to convince me that my spiritual path is wrong or evil. In fact, my mother once helped in the editing process for one of my books.

I think one of the reasons why my path never upset anyone in my family was because my great grandfather was involved in occult sciences in the 1800s. He was a medical doctor who was involved in the clinical uses of hypnosis. His book, *Mind and Body,* continues to be a standard reference source in the field of hypnotherapy. What was even more interesting was that he was one of the contributing authors to several occult journals of his day.

Working Solitary

Tim feels that working solitary is another important tradition within the Craft.

Many practitioners, for one reason or another, decide that practicing the Craft alone is for them. Some people live far from a circle or just feel that their spiritual path is one best explored alone, practiced on the solitary path.

Practicing Wicca alone is a very different experience from participating in a group. For starters, when you are alone, your celebrations and rituals can be as long or as short, as elaborate or as simple as you want them to be. You are free of the political rumblings that can often be part of group participation.

Many solitary practitioners are alone because they don't like Craft politics. Also, when you work alone, you might feel less inhibited to try new approaches and to explore more challenging spiritual work.

On the other hand, group energy and practice can lead to breakthrough spiritual experiences. If you have the opportunity to really train with a reputable group, I fully encourage it. Under the tutelage of an experienced Craft elder, you can have very powerful, directed, life-changing experiences.

11
GERINA DUNWICH

My life began in a very magickal way. My mother, who had difficulty bearing children and experienced three miscarriages, gave birth to me after wearing a fertility charm given to her by a gypsy. From the day of my birth forward, she has always referred to me as her "little Witchling."

As a child, I always felt that I was different from other children. I experienced both clairvoyant and paranormal phenomena at a young age. I had strange recurring nightmares about the Burning Times and found that I could make certain things happen simply by willing them to. I identified with Witches in movies and in books. Not one Halloween passed that I didn't parade proudly about the neighborhood with my black cape, pointed black hat, and straw broom.

The Courage We Need

Even when she was young, Gerina had the courage to stand up for her beliefs, even when it meant butting heads with people.

One Halloween when I was about 8 years old, a neighborhood girl who was out trick-or-treating with me sarcastically told me that she didn't think I looked like a "real" Witch because my face had not been painted green and I was not sporting an ugly wart-covered plastic nose.

I felt compelled to defend Witches and angrily informed her that real Witches were neither ugly nor evil and that anyone who thought so was just plain ignorant. She proceeded to taunt me and spew derogatory remarks about Witches until I became so furious I punched her right in the nose with all my might!

My mother was understandably upset that evening when the girl showed up at our front door with a broken nose, accompanied by her parents and a police officer. But no matter what I did, I was still my mother's little Witchling.

From these dynamic beginnings, Gerina continued her interest in Witches. Then a series of events began directing her towards the Wiccan spiritual path.

One of the biggest turning points in my life came in 1969. I was living in Illinois at the time, and my cousins Carol and Dave arrived from the West Coast to spend the summer at my grandmother's house. Carol was a few years older than I. She was a long-haired, free-spirited California hippie who smelled of patchouli oil and practiced Witchcraft. That summer, she turned me on to such things as spirit guides, animal familiars, and the workings of black, white, and gray magick.

My cousins and I also spent many hours using the Ouija board and conducting seances to successfully communicate with the spirits of the dead. One stormy night, Carol initiated me into the Craft. The secret, candlelit ceremony was held in my grandmother's attic amidst flashes of lightning and the rumble of thunder, and included the signing of a Witch's oath in blood. It was a very moving experience for me.

Summoning the Wind

In the early 1970s, I found myself drawn to a book that contained an old spell to summon the wind. Barefoot and bell-bottomed, I stood on the back steps of my parents' house in Illinois with my arms outstretched to the afternoon sky, chanting the ancient incantation over and over.

I can still remember the pounding of my young heart and the tingles that raced up and down my spine when I heard the rustling of leaves in the breeze and felt a gentle wind caressing my face.

I repeated the spell a number of times that Spring and was successful each time.

Gerina had a friend, Robert, who shared her interest in the occult and was most anxious to try his luck at the wind spell after she told him about it.

He came over to my house when my parents were away, and we began reciting the incantation in my backyard. The wind began to stir, and then it slowly grew stronger as we continued to chant. However, when the sky began to darken with ominous clouds that appeared to be forming into a funnel, we figured it was time to stop what we were doing.

Frantically, Gerina and Robert searched through the book to find some kind of a counterspell but could locate no instructions to undo the deadly storm they were convinced they had conjured up.

I could feel panic setting in when suddenly, as if being guided by someone or something from beyond, I instinctively began to repeat the chant backwards. I willed the spell to be undone.

After 10 or 15 minutes, which to me felt like an eternity, the winds finally calmed and, much to my relief, the clouds dissipated. That was the first and last time Robert and I performed magick together.

My Father's Abusive Ways

Having magickal experiences and turning the ordinary into the extraordinary is one of the things that being a Witch is all about. Stepping into these experiences rather than backing away from them takes courage, especially when it is so much easier to just turn and run. Although Gerina's mother was supportive of her daughter's spiritual beliefs, her father simply couldn't understand them.

My atheist father did not approve of any of my dabbling in the occult and was extremely upset when he discovered a fairly good-sized pentagram I had drawn on the garage floor in chalk one Halloween night.

When I was around 13 years old, he ransacked my bedroom and threatened to throw me out of the house after discovering my collection of spellbooks, a Voodoo doll, and some talismans that I kept hidden in a cabinet above my clothes closet. He ranted and raved and even accused me of using black magick to give him gout and a heart condition.

Ironically, he believed very strongly in the existence of magick and feared the occult, despite his atheistic views on religion.

In the mid-1970s, my parents' marriage came to a bitter end as the result of my father's abusive and adulterous behavior. My father took the stand in divorce court and, in a feeble attempt to gain sympathy, told the judge and the lawyers that he was a victim of the Black Arts. He claimed that I used my "powers of darkness" to render him ill and torment his sleep with nightmares on a regular basis. He even had the Voodoo doll to prove it.

Needless to say, the courtroom resounded with laughter, and my mother was awarded alimony, the house, and the car. I never saw my father again.

What Dreams May Come

Dreams often play an important part in pointing out our life path, particularly our spiritual path. In Gerina's case, her dreams led her into one of her most intense life-changing experiences.

Shortly after I moved to Salem, Massachusetts, with my soul mate in 1984, I experienced a prophetic dream in which a spirit in the form of Sybil Leek appeared before me. Sybil wore a long black cloak, and her entire body was surrounded by an iridescent blue aura. In a soft-spoken voice that had an almost motherly tone to it, she spoke to me and revealed that my destiny as a writer of the occult was outlined in the stars.

The dream-Sybil's words rang true when, four years later, Gerina wrote and published Candlelight Spells. *This marked the beginning of her successful career as an author of numerous books on Witchcraft and the magickal arts.*

Another life-changing experience for Gerina came with the "birth" of Coven Mandragora on Candlemas of 1996 and her role as its High Priestess.

During my years with the coven, I experienced some of the happiest and most magickal moments of my life. It deeply saddened me when the coven came to an end, but I will always be grateful for the many invaluable lessons and loving friendships it bestowed upon me. My fond memories of Coven Mandragora will live on forever.

My Connection with Isis and Bast

Many Wiccans feel a kinship with a particular tradition and use it as a springboard for their connection to the Divine. In Gerina's case it came around the age of 20, when she began studying ancient Egyptian mythology.

The mythology fascinated me greatly, and I felt a strong connection to the goddess Isis. In 1980, I began editing and publishing a Pagan literary journal, which I named *Golden Isis* in her honor.

My spiritual relationship with Isis lasted for many years. While working on a book called *Your Magickal Cat,* I found myself deeply drawn to another Egyptian goddess, Bast, who has since become my patron deity. I have invoked her in a number of rituals, including healings, amatory enchantments, and divinations. She is a great protectress as well as an avenger, and she watches over my feline familiars.

I would love to someday erect on my property a sacred temple to Bast patterned after the one in the sacred site of Bubastis (but on a smaller scale, of course). In addition to being a temple of magick and worship, it would serve as a refuge for all of the homeless cats in my neighborhood.

When talking about her influences, Gerina cites the books of such authors as Sybil Leek, Leo Louis Martello, Doreen Valiente, Raymond Buckland, and Paul Huson as all exerting a profound effect upon her spiritual path and magickal practices. In the early 1990s she found herself continually drawn to Wiccan spirituality, both as a writer and as a practitioner. Since then she has returned to her original path, which she classifies as "pre-Gardnerian traditional Witchcraft."

My Practice Today

I mainly practice my own magickal tradition called Bast-Wicca. Its name is derived from the ancient Egyptian cat-goddess Bast, and it incorporates elements of feline-oriented folk magick and felidomancy (feline divination). I believe that all cats possess powerful mystical energies. In my opinion as both a Witch and a cat-lover, they are the most psychic and magickal of all animals.

Gerina also performs an extensive amount of spellwork in the areas of herbal enchantments and candle-burning rituals, and she's been known to dabble now and then in various forms of ceremonial magick. Also, being part–Hopi Indian, she has also found herself drawn to some of the Native American forms of magick.

On the average, I would say I work magick about once or twice a week. People from all over the world write to me, asking me to cast spells for them. A love potion to win the heart of another and a spell to attract money are two of the most common requests I receive.

Every now and then, I am asked to do a healing ritual for someone, which I always do free of charge. Occasionally, I receive requests to cast hexes on people, which I do not honor. One time I actually received a letter from an inmate in a state penitentiary inquiring if there was a spell I could perform to help him break out of prison! He was quite serious about it and even offered to pay me a large sum of money for my magickal services once he was "on the outside." (I thought it best not to answer his letter.)

Discrimination Continues

Prejudice against Wiccans is similar to this country's discrimination against those who practice Judaism, Buddhism, or even Catholicism.

When I was a child I was ostracized and even physically assaulted in school because I was a Witch. In junior high, I had my long auburn hair set on fire during social studies class by a student sitting behind me who chanted, "Burn, Witch, burn!"

My classmates roared with laughter as I sprang from my desk, screaming and clutching what was left of my singed locks. Even the teacher had difficulty containing his laughter as he ordered the class to simmer down. I ran home from school with tears in my eyes and a burning anger in my heart. The situation at school eventually became completely unbearable.

Another time in Gerina's life when she was confronted with discrimination was when she was living in a rural region in upstate New York and decided to assemble a coven.

I had absolutely no contacts in the area so I figured the best way to connect was to advertise—discreetly, of course. I submitted a carefully worded ad to more than a half-dozen local newspapers, announcing that a study group was being formed for "like-minded individuals interested in ancient Goddess religions and Earth-centered spirituality."

The words *coven* and *Witch* were never mentioned. However, all but one of the newspapers refused, without any explanation whatsoever, to run my ad.

Today Gerina lives in the Los Angeles area, where many alternative lifestyles and spiritual practices are more accepted.

Because of who I am on a professional level, I am very discreet when it comes to revealing my identity, for the obvious reasons of safety and privacy. However, this is not to say that discrimination and religious intolerance are nonexistent here in the ultra-liberal City of Angels. I have a friend who is a well-known actress, and when word got around town that she was also a practicing Witch, she was not only ridiculed by some of her Hollywood peers, but people in the motion picture industry actually refused to hire her because they did not approve of her Pagan beliefs and practices.

Unfortunately, prejudice in this country continues. In the past it has been against Jews, Italians, Irish, Blacks, Asians, and Hispanics; now it is against Wiccans. Fortunately, because of the obvious legal consequences, Witches are no longer burned at the stake, but discrimination exists nonetheless. This is why individuals such as Gerina Dunwich should be commended for standing up for their beliefs. As the founding mothers and fathers who often came to the United States to escape the clutches of religious oppression did, modern Pagans, including Gerina and the other authors included in this book, are testing the boundaries of religious tolerance.

Why I Am Wiccan

I know that a large number of people, especially women and feminists, are drawn to Wicca because they feel empowered by a religion that deifies the feminine principle and treats the role of the female priestess as being equal in importance (or as being greater, in some traditions) to that of the male priest.

However, my involvement in Wicca had always been more on a magickal level than one having to do with feminism, politics, or even religion. What I find to be the most empowering aspect of the path I follow is the freedom that it allows for me to retain my individuality and to do my own thing without having to conform or adhere to any particular set of rules, ethics, traditions, or dogma other than those which my own heart chooses to follow.

I also feel that it is important for anyone who journeys down any spiritual path to be able to freely experiment, to grow, to change, and to think for one's self. In some religions, that is more than enough to get a person excommunicated.

Wicca is considered to be the fastest growing religion in the world today, and Gerina expects to see this trend continue in the future.

As the number of Wiccans increases throughout the world, I would also like to see a strengthening of unity taking place within the Wiccan community and less bickering, snobbery, and intolerance for the diverse spiritual, magickal, and occult traditions that exist outside of the Wiccan realm.

We need to remember that although we are all different, we are all as one. We must not allow our differences to divide us, lest we fail in our ongoing efforts to prevent the Burning Times from recurring.

Gerina attributes the increasing number of newcomers to Wicca to the visibility that Wicca has been given over the past few years by the Internet.

People are initially drawn to the Wiccan path for the same reasons they were more than 30 years ago when I first called myself a Witch. Some individuals become involved with Wicca or Witchcraft because they thirst for power over others or are desperate to have all of their problems instantly solved with the wave of a magick wand.

Many young people also see the Craft as a cool fad to follow or a way to get their kicks. These, of course, are all the wrong reasons to turn to Wicca (or any other spiritual path, for that matter).

On the other hand, there are the many folks who have embraced Wicca because they disagreed with and felt oppressed by the views and actions of the majority. Spiritually unfulfilled, the magickal lifestyle was written in the stars for them at the time of their birth.

I Prefer to Help Others

I've always been the type of Witch who prefers to use her healing energies to help others in need rather than herself. I've performed healings both in a coven environment and as a solitary practitioner.

When I first began doing healings, I worked primarily with crystals and gemstones, but as I experimented with other methods, I found candle magick and poppets to be much more effective.

Gerina has had some extraordinarily dramatic experiences doing magickal healings for others.

I recently received a request from a distraught woman whose husband had been diagnosed with a rare and deadly form of cancer. When the moon was right, I performed a long-distance healing ritual for him.

About two weeks later his wife wrote to me again, this time to express her heartfelt gratitude for my help. She informed me that shortly after my ritual work had been carried out, her husband returned to the hospital for some further tests. He felt as though he had been given a second chance at life when the bewildered doctors were unable to find any traces of the cancer in his body!

12 SKYE ALEXANDER

I grew up in the Bible Belt and knew from the time I was a very young child that my spiritual views were radically different from what the fundamentalist Christians around me preached.

I've always been a Pagan. From an early age, I experienced a strong affinity with Nature and animals, a keen intuition, an awareness of the spirit realm and a divine presence, and a strong sense of connectedness with all that exists in the heavens and on Earth.

When I was in my mid-30s and going through a very difficult time, I asked for help and instantly experienced what William Bucke called "cosmic consciousness": a complete sensory dissolution into a state of bliss, in which I lost all awareness of self, time, and the physical world. I was conscious only of divine love, of being surrounded and suffused with pink light, and of union with the all. Since then, I've never doubted the presence of the Goddess and her love for me.

The Magick of Personal Transformation

Skye had another powerful life-changing experience that demanded not only a great deal of courage, but also some plain old-fashioned magick. In the fall of 1999, she realized that her life was not as fulfilling as she wanted it to be. Yet she didn't know how or what to change about it.

Until 1999, I'd kept my Wiccan beliefs and magickal practice pretty quiet. But during that summer, I decided it was time for me to become more open and active with it. Within a few days of my decision, a person I knew (but not very well) whose beliefs were similar to mine showed up, literally, on my doorstep. The teacher appears when the student is ready, so it's said.

His friendship inspired me to explore magick more deeply and to live my beliefs more fully. In the process, I came to realize that I'd gotten stuck in a rut and that my life needed some updating.

Because I didn't know exactly what that entailed, I left the details up to the Goddess and began doing magick to become the person I truly wanted to be, to attract people who were right for me, and to live a life that was in harmony with Divine Will as well as my own true will.

I performed a variety of magickal rituals daily for a month with the intent of creating the life I truly wanted, becoming the person I truly wanted to be, and attracting people and circumstances into my life that were right for me—without knowing exactly what that would involve. By the end of the month, my life began to transform.

I never expected my entire, comfortable existence to come crashing down around me. Over the next few months, my marriage of 25 years broke up. I lost an entire network of friends, and encountered so many other problems with family, career, and finances, that my life began to sound like a bad country-western song.

The crisis undermined my trust, my security, and my sense of self-worth. Mired in my misery, I couldn't see that the Universe was telling me I'd "been there, done that" long enough. I needed to move on.

Yet even though I couldn't see where I was going, I kept doing my magick, kept asking for guidance, kept believing (although not always very strongly) that the Goddess would eventually lead me in the right direction.

She did. I now have a whole new circle of terrific friends, a wonderful lover, work I enjoy, and a beautiful home. I started painting again, signed a book contract with a new publisher, and openly began practicing my Wiccan beliefs with other people. But in order to create a new life that was right for me, the old one had to be torn down. I am much more content with my life than ever before.

Magick always works, but not necessarily in the way we expect or want it to. The key is to get out of the way and let it transpire—and to trust that what happens is for the best.

Living in Harmony with Divine Will

Magick has always been part of Skye's life.

Neo-Pagan and Wiccan spirituality appeal to be because they are harmonious with my Celtic heritage, my Aquarian dislike of rigid hierarchy, my feminist leanings, and my love of Nature. Wicca provides something of a framework, a validation if you will, for my worldview and way of existing in the world. I suppose I've always been a Witch, even when I didn't know what to call myself. Now I'm just open about it.

I'm a bit eclectic as I embrace Wiccan philosophy and celebrate the Sabbats. I also incorporate astrology, some Eastern yogic practices, Taoist and Buddhist meditations, feng shui, American Indian wisdom teachings, Shamanic journeying, and some Golden Dawn–style rituals into my magickal work.

Each morning I do the lesser banishing ritual of the Pentagram. I walk my labyrinth, light candles, and burn incense to send prayers to the Goddess. I regularly perform spells and rituals, concoct potions, and make mojos. I create magickal paintings, give offerings to the deities, and do sex magick. I celebrate the eight Sabbats with a group of other Witches, as well as marking them in solitary. I also do lunar magick and structure my professional and personal activities in connection with celestial cycles.

I feel I am in constant contact with the Divine. I see the Goddess's hand in everything and try to remain open to her guidance at all times. I pray ceaselessly and attempt to live in harmony with Divine Will. The goddesses to whom I feel most connected are Brigid and Kwan Yin, although others help me at certain times, too.

For me, Wicca's reverence for the Divine Feminine is most empowering especially to women, as most of us were raised under patriarchal belief systems.

I also feel it is important to reconnect with Nature and the heaven and Earth cycles—the Wheel of the Year—in this age of technology and scientism.

Knowing that we are co-creators with the Goddess, that we are the authors of our own destinies while also being part of a divine plan, and that our actions, thoughts, and feelings influence not only ourselves but others as well, is both empowering and humbling, in the most positive way.

Blending Wicca and Astrology

Skye has created—and practices—a unique blend of magick and astrology. Her book Magickal Astrology *explores this unique and effective combination.*

Having been an astrologer since the mid-1970s, I see life in terms of cosmic cycles and know that working with celestial energies can enhance just about anything, including magickal practice. The Sabbats, for example, are keyed to the sun's passage through the signs of the zodiac: The equinoxes and solstices occur on the days when the sun enters the cardinal signs Aries, Cancer, Libra, and Capricorn; the cross-quarter days fall at the halfway point between these dates.

As many Witches do, I tap into the moon's energies when doing spells and rituals. For instance, I perform magick intended to generate growth and expansion during the waxing moon. I cast spells that involve decrease or letting go during the waning moon.

I also consider the sign positions of the sun, moon, and planets in spellworking and choose celestial energies that are harmonious with the nature of the magick I'm doing. For instance, I have found that love spells are most successful when I do them when the sun and/or moon are in the Venus-ruled signs of Taurus and Libra and/or when Venus is well-placed by aspect and sign. I also work love spells during the day (Friday) and hour (sixth hour of the day) that are ruled by Venus.

I do most of my magickal work in my backyard labyrinth. The classic, seven-circuit "Pagan" labyrinth has one circuit for each of the heavenly bodies that we can see with the naked eye. Therefore, the labyrinth is a symbolic embodiment of the cosmos and the energies of the celestial bodies and can be tapped into by walking through their corresponding circuits. I've found that performing rituals and spells within this ancient pattern increases their power and effectiveness. I even created an astrological labyrinth ritual that I use.

The Healing Power of Wicca

I have experienced the healing power of Wicca many times. All my life, I'd suffered with intensely painful menstrual cramps. The first time I did sex magick, my cramps disappeared and have never returned.

I don't do healing work with a group or coven. Occasionally, I do healing for other people, if asked, mostly to relieve pain.

I think it's positive overall to make people aware of Wicca, because openness and familiarity help to reduce the fear factor. It also provides young people, especially young women, with a spiritual path that respects the feminine and enables them to get the information they need to make appropriate choices for themselves.

Skye feels that Wicca gives us a way to recognize, respect, and reconnect with the Divine Feminine as well as the personal feminine.

I think many women have rejected patriarchal religions and turned to Wicca because it honors them rather than demeaning or discounting them. In addition, I think the overemphasis on science and technology has caused us to feel alienated from the world in which we live. Wicca enables us to experience ourselves as part of Nature and the cosmos.

In the future, Skye hopes to be able to play a larger role in the Wicca Movement.

Wicca is currently fashionable, a trend of sorts, and I expect some of its present popularity will fade, but it will remain much stronger than it has been in the past. After all, the people who have seriously embraced Wicca and Pagan spirituality aren't likely to relinquish it or return to the beliefs they were raised with.

MARION WEINSTEIN

I think women understand that traditional religions don't serve them. When I started being a public Witch in the early 1960s, feminists were very condescending to us. They didn't understand. They thought religion was the opiate of the masses, no matter what religion it was. All religion was bad. Now, they finally realize and think women's spirituality is the best thing in the world.

*Marion Weinstein was on radio for 13 years and one of the first people to publish a book on Witchcraft (*Positive Magic: Occult Self-Help*). Being a public Witch early on caused problems with her sisters, to the point that she just says, "Things have gotten ugly." These and other problems have not stopped Marion from following her chosen spiritual path, even if it hasn't been the most popular thing to do.*

Since publishing her first book, Marion has written a number of books, including Earth Magic *and* Marion Weinstein's Handy Guide to the I Ching. *She has also recorded a series of audiotape workshops. As with many of the other individuals in this book, she has exhibited, and continues to exhibit, the courage that makes this country and the Wicca Movement great.*

A Divine Experience

One of Marion's more amazing experiences occurred when she was on the radio. Five nuns in a convent on Staten Island called into the radio program to tell her that they all had converted to Witchcraft.

I was an out-of-the-closet Witch on radio programs in the early 1970s. I had a radio show on WBAI in New York City called "Marion's Cauldron" that was a combination talk show/interview show, with a heavy emphasis on magick, Wicca, and the Goddess.

WBAI always had a highly political atmosphere, charged with liberalism, feminism, everything left wing, and power to every conceivable minority. Yet it took years before my fellow and sister radio hosts finally accepted my on-air work as meaningful.

The listeners were a different story. They were enormously accepting from the start. Even the skeptics told me they enjoyed my stories and jokes.

I did numerous shows about the Goddess, which was still a new idea to most people at the time. I knew who my listeners were through on-the-air phone calls and letters. But this was just the tip of the iceberg. I sensed the silent presence of tens of thousands of people out there who never wrote or called. Yet, I knew they were listening.

After doing about 13 years of radio, one day I answered a phone call off the air. Sometimes the phones were still lit up after I signed off, but I always tried to answer everyone before I went home. This time, it was a woman's voice, someone new.

She said, "Marion, I want you to know I'm an ex-nun."

"No kidding," I said. "And you listen to my show?"

She replied, "We all did at the convent. And we want you to know something. We listened every week."

I said, "That's great. And you all still listen?"

She answered, "Yes, but we're not at the convent any more. We all left and became Witches."

I still get shivers when I think about this conversation. I never expected or suspected anything like this in a million years. I told her that my intention was never to convert.

She said, "Oh, it wasn't you. You provided the information of course, but it was our own idea. Two of us are married now."

She sounded so very happy. I asked where the convent was, and she told me Staten Island.

The people in charge at the convent never knew exactly what happened, why so many nuns left at the same time. I'm not sure how many. I recall she said five, but it could have been more.

Portrait of a Young Witch

I was raised Jewish and started out by studying the Cabala. In Judaism there is questioning. It wasn't that hard to be a Jewish Witch, not that hard at all. The mood was true, but not the God concept.

I always knew I was a Witch. I used to dress up my bulldogs as Witches, and Halloween was my favorite holiday. My parents didn't know, and I didn't tell them until I was in college.

When I was a little girl, I was fascinated by prayer and even more so by magick. I don't mean the magician and top hat kind; I mean the stories about Fairy godmothers and Witches. I somehow suspected that the Witches in those old tales were seriously misrepresented.

I must have had memories from other lives: bonfires, dancing, flickering shadows. I loved candlelight and darkness. I dressed my dolls up as Witches. Needless to say, I was an anomaly amongst my childhood friends.

In a play at day camp, when I was 9, I was given the part of the Fairy godmother in Cinderella. I carried a magick wand my mother made for me, topped with a five-pointed star. In the play, I saved the day with magick. It felt familiar and right.

Her first magickal experience took place on a full moon when Marion was about 13.

I stepped outside myself and realized there was power in that experience. It just blew my mind. I didn't know how to channel it, didn't know what to do with it, but knew it was sacred. Standing inside the circle, I felt powerful. At that moment I realized anything was possible. That moment touched my heart and left an impression on me.

I had the philosophy of Witchcraft without knowing it when I was young. In high school, I learned how to do research. I researched old fairy tales, looking for the truth. I traced the legend of Mother Goose back to Charlemagne's mother, the goose-footed queen—a lady who told magickal tales that were all based on true stories.

With this, I realized that legends were true, and that magick was real. I experienced a rush of flashes and memories. The floodgates had opened.

I devoted my life to the Wiccan path at 15. I knew there was a basis for magick, and I was going to dedicate my life to it. Magick was taken out of our culture in the 14th century. I believe it's my job to help bring it back.

Establishing A Coven

Marion's friends evolved into her coven. It provided, and still provides her with a support group. Even though some coven members have moved to other parts of New York, they still work by phone.

One of Marion's most magickal experiences came the first time her coven met.

I had been working with candles for many years, but in 1970, we actually formed our coven. When we sat down to figure out our rituals, we had to figure out how to pass the candle from person to person and to work with each person while visualizing a castle. It was amazing. This was my first ritual experience, and it was binding type of memory. It created a very strong connection between the members.

Finding a group of people I could relate to gave me a sense of purpose and a religion that I could live and believe in, rather than searching or trying to live up to some sainted religion that I was born into. I felt very fulfilled spiritually and had a practical tool for daily life. Sometimes magick doesn't act in the way or time frame you lay out, but nonetheless, it works. Intention and purpose are what make magick work.

All the Divine Help I Can Get

I am an eclectic Wiccan, and my group and I developed our own methods. I called myself Dianic before this was considered separatist. Diana is still my primary alignment with the Goddess, and I work with many aspects of her. I was born on the new moon, which I believe is Diana's territory.

I used to just work with Diana, but now I work with all aspects of the Goddess and God. I have since added Selene, Kernunnos, and Pan. I work with different pantheons because I need all the divine help I can get when I do magick.

Every day I do works of power, and I continually work with the I Ching. I call in the four corners every morning and do rituals and spells according to my needs, particularly if there's a problem or I need a healing. Basically, I practice magick in everything I do. I cared for my mom for 20 years in her old age, and I did a lot of work for health and safety. She was very accepting and became a Witch, which was a very affirming experience.

Search and Rescue

Sometimes I use my magickal skills to find things. I once found a lost child. My friend was visiting and had brought her child, and the child disappeared. Everyone was frantic. I lit a candle, and I saw him standing next to a pylon on the beach. I knew where it was so I went to the spot and there he was. His parents were very happy.

Rescue work has become a mainstay of Marion's life on the Wiccan path.

My first familiar was a little poodle whose name was Muffin. When Muffin died, I vowed that I would give help in any way I could to any animal that came across my path and needed it. I find homes for cats and dogs. (Yes, it is sometimes my own home.) I do animal rescue, and several animals have reincarnated to me several times. I've been doing rescue work for about 15 years, ever since I found a kitten.

Group Healing Rituals

When our coven gets together, we lay the circle, call in the wards, and manifest divine protection. We work with candles and visualize the animal or person as being completely healed. All the members see cells coming together, organs shifting, and bones mending. We try to get very specific. We even try to do what one of my friends calls psychic surgery (using focused psychic energy to remove blockages or disease from the body, mind, and spirit).

The most profound healing experience occurred when I was on vacation with two people from my coven, one of whom knew of someone whose son had a brain tumor. We met on the next full moon on the beach, where we drew down the moon and directed energy towards this child, whom we didn't know. Afterwards, he had complete recovery. That was a life-changing experience for me.

Creating the Invisible Castle

English Witches build an invisible castle, which they go into to do their work. Marion told her coven about this, and everyone immediately wanted to do it.

Now we use this technique all the time. The walls of the castle are lined with "no harmful power" and "for the good of all." All the work we do in the castle is according to Threefold Law. The castle has many rooms. It has a healing room and a healing fountain, as well as other healing aspects and beings in it.

Lately I have been doing weight loss in the castle. I visualize myself in the castle being thin and feeling great. I've lost 82 pounds, and because of this I'm now writing a Witchcraft diet book. It took me three years to get where I wanted to be.

The Witchcraft diet book also has meditations that you do before you eat anything. It helps you choose the right foods. Instead of *planning* to do it, you find yourself *doing* it. The method is tailored to your needs and who you are.

Because of psychological reasons, there are certain areas of your life that don't respond to magick. You have many background reasons for the problems you have, without blame or guilt as to who is responsible. You take that area and challenge to make it into a magickal area without getting discouraged. You create and manifest yourself according to your intention and desire. It is important that your intention be clear.

Wicca Is the Religion of the Future

Marion thinks it's wonderful that Witchcraft is going mainstream, but at the same time, she gets tired of the superficiality, gossiping, and backbiting.

I often wonder if these people are Witches. I don't think they understand the work, or they wouldn't be doing that. If you understand the way magick works, you can't do anything negative. Wicca is the religion of the future.

I don't go around announcing it in my daily life, so a lot of people don't know I'm a Witch. I live in New York where there are so many diverse people that no one cares if you're a Witch. I have always pretty much lived in New York, fairly close to the city. Currently I'm about 45 minutes outside the city. I used to want to be in the heart of the city, but now I've been connecting more to Nature, which strengthens my connection to the Divine.

Marion credits the Aquarian Age for having a lot to do with the current popularity of Witchcraft.

The environment also has a lot to do with it. Many people practice magick and Witchcraft, even if they don't know they are doing so. In particular, if they are environmentalists, then that's what they are doing.

The Wicca Movement will continue to become more integrated into society. It is becoming more accepted by the popular media everyday, and more men are embracing it. Witchcraft is becoming more a part of the culture, rather than being separate from it. How we put the information forward is very important.

I don't like groups that have a rigid way of doing things and don't allow for any other way of doing things. I think it's important to keep the spontaneity—after all, this is a folk religion that evolved over time. It's not something separate, but a part of daily life. Paganism was about the crops in the field. It's the religion of the people, which is more felt than thought.

14

Z. Budapest

My first magickal experience was my grandmother's death when I was 3 years old. It was shortly after World War II. We had no food to eat and no clean water to drink. Grandmother was starving. Before I was sent out to the countryside, where there was some food to eat, she gave us all her gold, rings, and necklaces—even her wedding ring—because only gold could buy food. She blessed me and then produced a red apple from underneath her pillow. She said she was saving it for my birthday.

Five days later, on an unusually warm afternoon, I was playing alone in the yard of our new apartment. My mother was in the house sleeping. I was playing funeral. I was playing red. I ground up some red bricks. Then I found some cotton balls and dipped them in the red. The white cotton turned to red. I remember liking them. I made more of the red cotton balls and put them all over the low bushes in the garden. I hung them all over the sunny garden, on the grass, and in the trees. It was a red garden. There were big red cotton balls all over the garden like blooms.

I felt content yet restless. I wondered, *What now?* I was finished doing the red game.

I suddenly heard my name called in the clear voice of my grandmother. "Zsuzsika! Zsuzsika!" I looked up, and from above, I saw her descending towards me. I wasn't surprised. She embraced and kissed me. She held me, and said sadly, "Poor little one. You won't have your dear granny anymore."

I was alarmed. "But why not?" I asked her. She cried and then hugged and kissed me more. The feelings of those hugs were like desperate fingers enclosing me.

I looked at her face. "Don't cry," I told her.

She let go of me. A forced smile was on her face and she faded like a cloud. She vanished.

I stood there and I understood. Death had come to meet me with my grandmother. I had already seen death plenty by then. I was born a year before the war broke out. But this was personal. Death took my granny, and she came to say good-bye.

I ran to my mother, who had already awakened. She was looking for me. I ran straight into her and announced, "I won't have my dear grandmother anymore!"

My mother knew, too. We both cried.

The red garden fit this scene so well. My mother looked at it and shook her head. She said to me, "Oh, no! You too!" That said it all. We were both now outcasts.

As my mother has, I have always seen things. She was often friends with the departed. She used to say that they made the best of friends. The dead were not fickle. They kept their word. The dead were honorable.

We found out much later, when the mail finally reached us, that it was at that very hour that Granny died.

I didn't know this was my first ritual, but it was: a meeting with the dead, at the hour of my grandmother's death. I saw how the dead were really alive, just in another dimension. Nobody could lie to me or scare me with death anymore, because I now knew that everybody we loved and cared for was alive on the other side.

Still, I managed to forget about this day. I pushed it aside. *No need to obsess,* I thought, so I moved on.

I moved across the world. I changed languages. Many years went by. Then around my young Crone time, I started remembering childhood scenes. This memory was there, fresh as ever: the memory of my first ritual.

A Witch without Knowing It

I really didn't know that I was a Witch for a long time. My mother was a psychic artist who sculpted goddesses. We prayed to the ancestors on the winds. I naturally thought everybody did.

It was only later when Z. was in first grade with the nuns that she found out about the existence of other religions.

Even then I best related to the saints, with their miracles. In particular, I loved the Hungarian saint Elizabeth, the queen's daughter who was charitable, and Margaret, another princess who lived with nuns on the isle of St. Margaret (then called the Island of the Rabbits).

When my mother had people come to the house for advice, or when she talked to me about meeting the dead in her dreams, it began to slowly dawn on me who we were. Even then I didn't know that what we practiced had anything to do with Wicca. At the time, I didn't know English. However, the Celts and the Hungarians lived together for a few hundred years and their intermingling produced a mutual influence, such as calling on the four corners and the V-center.

What I Know Now

Wicca is the belief system in many gods and goddesses, the intentionality of prayers, herbology, and magickal cures. These are all part of the tradition of my country. I would like to state that I have never read Mr. Gardner, and now I make it a point not to do so. Women's Mysteries do not come from him.

In terms of the Women's Mysteries, I was particularly influenced by Jane Harrison. In my writings and practice I have fused folk art, folk dances, and folk prayers with Celtic traditions and nomad customs. A lot of the information is from Jane Harrison, the noted professor from Oxford who spoke 20 languages and collected many sacred artifacts from the Mediterranean. I am referring to the women's festivals, particularly those that were lost to us until she unearthed them.

How I Practice

I used to pray to the many aspects of the Goddess, but nowadays I have returned to origins of all Goddesses, the Three Fates (Energy, Matter, and Meaning): Urd, Verdandi, and Sculd. I address these destiny deities about everything. It seems to work well.

Casting spells is good and fine, but what will be will be. You cannot spell your way out of destiny. I light candles every night. I pray twice a day. My spirit prays when I'm in Nature walking or just watching the sun set. I am a night person. My relationship with the Goddesses, all three of them, is very close. It's like consulting friends every day. I do not forget that life and living is the best prayer. I live every part of my life with passion.

My First Group Ritual and Beyond

My first group ritual was in my small apartment in Holly-wood on the Winter Solstice in 1971. We had done the best we could. We used a hibachi for a cauldron. We gathered to-gether a very diverse group of women, not all of whom were Witch material. This was my very first High Priestess service, and I was green. But my intention was to create a Women's Spirituality with the essence of common sense. One of three women went into trance and rhymed for four hours as the Otter Woman. We had others think of her as a freak. I prayed for Women's Spirituality to transform the world.

After a while, we noticed that it was raining. We all ran out, still holding hands, to catch the raindrops. This is when I noticed an owl in the palm Tree. My Goddess, an owl hooting in the rain is very unusual in Hollywood! Because it's a pro-phetic bird, I asked the owl for prophecy. I asked, "Is this experience tonight just for us or is it for the whole world? Hoot seven times if it's for the whole world, five times if it's a just for us." The owl hooted exactly seven times. I was so impressed. I knew then that we had started a movement that reached be-yond all of us who were present at this birthing. I was so high from that experience that I didn't need sleep for days.

Doing things for the first time doesn't allow for an initia-tion by a community that still needs to be built. I was first on the scene with my vision of Women's Spirituality. I did not invent Women's Spirituality. Rather, I have revived it. I re-claimed Women's Mysteries from the mists of time. They are mysteries that were last performed in the fifth century, before the Christians destroyed the temples of Elusis and salted the earth so nothing could grow there.

I grew from that soil and the well-tended temples with their earthen floors. I grew from the myths of Demeter and Kore, which my mother often sculpted with her two hands. So it's hard to say who or what initiated me. Sometimes people are born to bring in a certain consciousness that nobody can yet imagine.

I have circled with women on the Malibu mountaintops for 10 years. I passed down the community to Ruth Barrett. She led the circles for another 15 years, celebrating side by side with the seasons. She has passed it to Leticia, who is presently working with the growing community. I have ordained nine priestesses. I have written about my circles in my books, *Grandmother of Time* and *Grandmother Moon, Goddess in the Office, Goddess in the Bedroom,* and finally *Summoning the Fates.*

My vision still holds. Women must take back religion, traditions, culture, and all the expressions of spirituality. Social changes occur when women raise their consciousness. Nothing is as powerful to bring in the Aquarian Age. When women change, the world has changed.

Wicca and Family

My mother cooperated with me on the *Holy Book Of Women's Mysteries.* She turned over her collection of spells. She also collected superstitions that are remnants of old spells and beliefs that are now antiquated. She used to say, "Superstitions are for Christians, not Witches."

I have two sons and a grandson. My boys only practiced magick when they wanted girls to pay attention to them. As soon as the girlfriend issue was settled, they didn't practice anymore. My second son, who was born on Halloween, created a birthday ritual where he tossed a pumpkin off the highest point of the roof. Then we all gathered and practiced augury from how the pumpkin was smashed. He developed a whole mythology around his pumpkin ritual. The basis of it was that the god Fester sleeps and wakes up on Halloween. Unless we hit him on the head with a blessed pumpkin, he might wake up, and we would all disappear, because we are creatures in his dreams. It was fun. My son is now a scientist with a biotech firm.

I believe that one of the benefits of spirituality is that it helps us feel connected to our ancestors, to our entire line of ancestors.

Watching the Seeds Grow

Spirituality puts a good, solid perspective on one's life and hence provides peace of mind. I have practiced ritual magick always with a women's circle. We spelled for big things: world peace, protection for animals and wildlife, and the liberation of women. I have seen many social changes actually come true.

But these things take more time. I have also spelled for health and healing for others and have seen things improve. But no Witch is able to spell herself out from under normal occurrences that befall human beings. I discourage women from expecting a trouble-free life just because they are good Witches.

The archetypes of Witches are coming back in droves, and I am happy for all of them. Harry Potter, bless J. K. Rowling, is fabulous in bringing the conception of Witches into positive culture. But even the negative ones are fun. I enjoy them all, the more the better. I adored Samantha

Stephens. Sabrina is a hoot. It's beside the point if they are accurate or not. They are fun and they are powerful. That's the important thing.

Z. has always had a deep love of writing. When she started out, she just wanted to become a great Hungarian novelist.

We plan, and they finish. I am happy with how the Fates have used me. People in the United States needed a genetic Witch who is not afraid of sharing forbidden knowledge. Because of this I became a nonfiction writer. Blessed be.

Since my childhood, I have always known that I'd be a writer. After having written six books about women's spirituality, I have now written my first fiction book, *Rasta Dogs.* It's an animal advocacy book that promotes the humane treatment and understanding of animals. It's about my little dog Zoro (a Puli), who works in San Francisco at a mental health treatment center.

All of my works are steeped in Goddess consciousness, some more than others. I have also finished my third screenplay, *Sensitive Attila,* a fantasy/comedy. I am also producing a Goddess festival in 2002. It's a biannual event contemplating our place on the circle of rebirth. I am adding a Goddess Family Festival in 2003 for all of our children and loved ones.

I spent my youth trying to teach and incite. Now in my Cronehood, I watch the seeds grow, with new teachers taking on the mantle of High Priestess. Finally, I get to write fiction. My fates unfold into the third-Crone destiny now. I am excited and grateful for the journey.

AFTERWORD

Those who are courageous will be able to keep alive the spirit of individualism and dissent that gave birth to this country. We, as Wiccans, are just such a group of courageous people. We are a living, growing, and inspiring movement of ideas and practices that can help heal and reconnect us. Our courage and perseverance will be rewarded, and the wisdom of honoring the Earth will ultimately provide a more positive and healthy future for hundreds of generations to come.

Join the Spiritual Revolution!

We are born, live, and die. Governments rise and fall. But ideas live on. Ideas are immortal. Wiccan ideas have the most power and the most magick—the idea of working in harmony with the Earth, and the Elements, and each other, instead of competing with everything and everyone. Wicca is a spiritual revolution, one that encourages cooperation and forward-thinking, not the status quo or violence. It is a celebration of freedom, signifying renewal and rebirth as well as change.

Any time you go against the grain and push the envelope of what is permissible—as Wicca does—there are those who will oppose your efforts. In the relatively short history of humankind, many generations have been granted the role of changing things that don't work and of defending personal freedom when our rights are in grave jeopardy of being taken from us. As Wiccans, we need not shrink away from this responsibility; we must embrace it with all the divine power we can muster together.

As most everyone agrees, it's an extremely exciting time to be alive. I wouldn't change places with anyone of any other generation. The faith, energy, and magick that we gather together and carry into the world right now will light our lives, our county, and the universe in the years to come. That brilliance can light the universe!

Today, we have the power and resources to abolish all poverty and famine, as well as the technological power to destroy all forms of life, including people. I, for one, refuse to witness or permit the destruction of Mother Earth or the slow undoing of our basic human rights and the constitutional freedoms of speech and religion—rights and freedoms that our country has always been committed to.

Our rights can be no greater than our responsibilities. The protection of our civil and spiritual rights will continue to grow in strength as long as we continue to take responsibility for ourselves and our Goddess- and God-given freedoms.

Chart a Positive Course

Instead of focusing on the differences between religions, or on the Burning Times, and instead of belaboring the problems that divide us, we need to fix the course for a more positive future and focus on what unites us. United, we shall overcome difficult challenges and do many good works in a host of cooperative efforts. Divided and split asunder, Wiccans can do very little to promote our ideas and practices.

It is time to transform our good words into good deeds in our homes, in our communities, in our country, and around the world. The Internet is the perfect ambassador for Wiccans who want to connect with other Wiccans across the globe. With the Internet it becomes possible to unlock the shackles of fear and prejudice, to unite as one people who are willing to create a better future—a future filled with peace instead of violence, creative thought and communication instead of corporate oppression and alienation, and love instead of hate.

Let us begin anew—remembering that civility, compassion, and truth are signs of strength, not weakness, in the Wiccan Movement. Let us truly invoke the wonders of magick. Each one of us is in a position of responsibility. Our future depends on how we fulfill our responsibilities. There will be times when you must do what you must do regardless of the consequences, dangers, and pressures, and that is the basis for all human morality.

Imagine the Best!

I dare each of you to imagine the best world you can and to think about the possibilities of the freedom and future of humankind. With divine communion as our only sure reward and with time as the final witness of our words and deeds, it is time to go out into the world and share our ideas, spiritual teachings, and practices. It's time to ask for the blessing of the Goddess and God and for their divine help, love, and protection.

As I sit here on Beltane 2001, finishing this book, the United States was just kicked out of the United Nations Commission on Human Rights, after being part of the Commission since its inception in 1947. The basis for the dismissal was some of the Bush administration's policies, including the opposition to the Kyoto Proposal and the insistence on missile defense. This is the wrong direction for our nation to be heading. I am an advocate of world peace and abhor any kind of war. We need to uphold human rights and stop the violence, not create more of it. This is especially relevant right now, considering the tragic shootings and killings in American schools. As one people, we need to address the world issues of hunger, poverty, overpopulation, slavery, and global warming, not shy away from them. We need to create brotherhood and sisterhood among the many nations of this Earth, instead of digging a deep dry well of hate and intolerance.

Everything today seems so twisted around and haywire. When did the truth, compassion, and a helpful hand become bad things? When did they get cast aside? I always have loved the story about Truth and Falsehood, where Truth decided to go naked instead of donning Falsehood's clothing. It's time that we as a people embrace a more truthful and "skyclad state of mind." As William Blake wrote, "If the lens of perception were cleansed, then all would be as it is, infinite."

Are We Ready?

I, as did many before me, thirst for a Golden Age, a Magickal Age and a new era of tolerance, where world peace and understanding exist. My childhood was spent getting under my school desk in case of nuclear attack, watching the president of my country being gunned down, and seeing my own family dissolve into divorce, so I welcome the idea of a

Golden Age. I know that we as Wiccans, as a group, can turn bad news into good news and transform negativity into positive change.

I challenge each one of you to make a positive change, to embrace the miracle of life every moment. Be bold and courageous enough to stand up for what you believe, to seek the magick out, and to bring it into your daily life. And remember to share the magick with others, with your children, and with your children's children. Share the ideas that make Wicca such a divine spiritual revolution. It's essential that we stay on track and follow the Pagan path, a path that will lead us back in harmony with Mother Earth and back in harmony with ourselves and one another.

Wicca is a religion founded by independent forward-thinkers. It is a spiritual path for dreamers and for those who hear a different drummer, one that plays in step with the heart-beat of Mother Earth. Wicca is a spirituality that welcomes those individuals who have profound faith in personal freedom, faith in the power of truth, justice, and liberty for all.

We are one world, one people, under the naked eyes of the Goddess and God. In the words of President John F. Kennedy, "Our most basic common link is that we all inhabit this small planet. We all breathe the same air. We all cherish our children's futures. And we are all mortal."

Let us all remember his words of wisdom as we usher the Wiccan Movement into the 21st century.

Appendix

INTERNET AND
BOOKS LISTINGS

The following is a listing of the popular Wiccan authors who are included in this book, together with their Internet sites and the books they have written. The author listings correspond with the order in which they appear in the book.

I encourage readers who are interested in Wicca and magick to look through, and hopefully read, as many of these books as possible. The books listed are filled with hands-on information from veteran practitioners and reputable Wiccan authors, and are certain to bring a little more magick into your life. If you have any questions or would like more information, please contact the author directly at her or his Internet site.

Sirona Knight

www.sironaknight.com
www.dcsi.net/~bluesky

Books

A Witch Like Me
The Witch And Wizard Training Guide
Exploring Celtic Druidism
The Wiccan Web
The Little Giant Encyclopedia of Runes
*Dream Magic: Night Spells and Rituals for Love,
    Prosperity, and Personal Power*
*Celtic Traditions: Druids, Faeries, and Wiccan
    Rituals*
Love, Sex, and Magick
The Pocket Guide to Crystals and Gemstones
The Pocket Guide to Celtic Spirituality
The Shapeshifter Tarot
Moonflower: Erotic Dreaming with the Goddess
Greenfire: Making Love with the Goddess
Solstice Shift (Contributing Author)

Forthcoming Books

The Cyber Spellbook
Faery Magick
Goddess Bless!
Practical Wicca

Contributing Editor for *Magical Blend* magazine
P.O. Box 600
Chico, CA 95928
www.magicalblend.com

Dorothy Morrison

www.geocities.com/Athens/Olympus/8774/

Books

Enchantments of the Heart
*Bud, Blossom, and Leaf: A Magical Herb
    Gardener's Handbook*
The Whimsical Tarot
Yule: A Celebration of Light and Warmth
*In Praise of the Crone: A Celebration of Feminine
    Maturity*
Everyday Magic
Magical Needlework

Patricia "Trish" Telesco

www.loresinger.com

Books

Exploring Candle Magick
A Charmed Life
Gardening with the Goddess
A Witch's Beverages and Brews
The Wiccan Web
Magic Made Easy
Spinning Spells, Weaving Wonders
The Language of Dreams
Ghost, Spirits, and Hauntings
The Little Book of Love Magic
The Kitchen Witch's Cookbook
Your Book of Shadows
Advanced Wicca
Goddess in My Pocket
Shaman in a 9-5 World
365 Goddesses
The Wiccan Book of Ceremonies and Rituals

Victorian Grimoire
The Healer's Handbook
The Herbal Arts
Cat Magic
Dog Spirit
Seasons of the Sun
Wishing Well
Magickal Places
Futuretelling
The Magic of Folk Wisdom
Wicca 2000
Mirror, Mirror
How To Be A Wicked Witch
Sacred Patterns
Through the Year: 365 Days of Prosperity
A Floral Grimoire
Brother Wind, Sister Rain
The Urban Pagan
The Victorian Flower Oracle
Folkways: Reclaiming the Magic and Wisdom
A Witch's Brew

A.J. Drew

www.neopagan.com

Books

Wicca Spellcraft For Men
Wicca For Men

Owner of Salem West
Columbus, Ohio

Phyllis Currot

www.witchcrafting.org
www.bookofshadows.com

Books

Witch Crafting: A Spiritual Guide to Making Magic
Book Of Shadows: A Woman's Journey Into the Wisdom of Witchcraft

Raven Grimassi

www.stregheria.com

Books

The Encyclopedia of Wicca and Witchcraft
The Wiccan Mysteries: Ancient Origins and Teachings
Ways of the Strega
Italian Witchcraft: The Old Religions of Southern Europe
Hereditary Witchcraft: Secrets of the Old Religion
Wiccan Magick: Inner Teachings of the Craft

Editor of
Raven's Call: A Journal of Modern Wicca, Witchcraft, and Magick
P.O. Box 22349
San Diego, CA 92192

Owner of Raven's Loft
Escondido, California

Silver RavenWolf

> *www.silverravenwolf.com*

Books

> *To Ride A Silver Broomstick*
> *To Stir A Magick Cauldron*
> *To Light a Sacred Flame*
> *Angels: Companions in Magick*
> *American Folk Magick: Charms, Spells, and*
>   *Herbals*
> *Teen Witch Kit*
> *Silver's Spells for Prosperity*
> *Silver's Spells for Protection*
> *Silver's Spells for Love*
> *Halloween!: Customs, Recipes, and Spells*
> *Teen Fiction Books*
> *Teen Witch*
> *Teen Witch Kit*
> *Beneath A Mountain Moon*
> *Murder at Witches Bluff*
> *Witches Night Out*
> *Witches Night of Fear*
> *Witches Key to Terror*

Raymond Buckland

> *www.geocities.com/SoHo/Workshop/6650*

Books

> *Gypsy Witchcraft and Magic*
> *Gypsy Fortune Telling Tarot Kit*
> *Advanced Candle Magick*
> *Cardinal's Sin*
> *Ray Buckland's Magic Cauldron*
> *Buckland Gypsies' Domino Divination Deck*
> *Truth About Spirit Communication*
> *The Committee*

*Doors to Other Worlds: A Practical Guide to
    Communicating with Spirits*
Scottish Witchcraft
The Book of African Divination
Secrets of Gypsy Love Magick
Witchcraft Yesterday and Today
Secrets of Gypsy Fortunetelling
Secrets of Gypsy Dream Reading
Buckland's Complete Book of Witchcraft
Practical Color Magick
Witchcraft from the Inside
Practical Candleburning Rituals
The Magic of Chant-O-Matics
Anatomy of the Occult
Amazing Secrets of the Psychic World
Here Is the Occult
The Tree: Complete Book of Saxon Witchcraft
Mu Revealed (As Tony Earll)
Witchcraft Ancient and Modern
A Pocket Guide to the Supernatural
Witchcraft: The Religion

Raymond Buckland's Museum
Preview at *www.angelfire.com/wi/monte/museum.html*

Lady Sabrina

users.aol.com/LadyS13661/books.htm

Books

*Exploring Wicca: The Beliefs, Rites, and Rituals of
    the Wiccan Religion*
*The Witch's Master Grimoire: An Encyclopedia of
    Charms, Spells, Formulas, and Magickal Rites*
Secrets of Modern Witchcraft Revealed
Cauldron of Transformation
Reclaiming the Power

Timothy Roderick

www.earthdancecollective.org

Books

Apprentice to Power
Dark Moon Mysteries
The Once Unknown Familiar

Gerina Dunwich

www.wicca.drak.net/dunwich
clubs.yahoo.com/clubs/gerinadunwichscauldron
iamawitch.com/freepages/grimoire
clubs.yahoo.com/clubs/paganpoetssociety
E-mail: witchywoman13@usa.net

Books

Exploring Spellcraft
The Pagan Book of Halloween
Your Magickal Cat
Magick Potions
Wicca A To Z
A Wiccan's Guide to Prophecy and Divination
Everyday Wicca
The Wicca Source Book
The Wicca Garden
The Wicca Book of Days
The Wicca Spellbook
Wicca Love Spells
Wicca Craft
Circle of Shadows
The Concise Lexicon of the Occult
Wicca Candle Magick
Candlelight Spells

Skye Alexander

www.shore.net/~mojo
E-mail: mojo@shore.net

Books

Magickal Astrology
Hidden Agenda
Planets in Signs

Monthy magickal astrology articles in *Magical Blend*
www.magicalblend.com

Marion Weinstein

www.earthmagic.com
E-mail: marion@earthmagic.com

Books

Earth Magic
Positive Magic: Occult Self-Help
Marion Weinstein's Handy Guide to Tarot Cards
Marion Weinstein's Handy Guide to the I Ching
Worskhops on Tape
Tarot Cards
The I Ching
Words of Power
Beyond the Leaves

Z. Budapest

www.zbudapest.com

Books

The Holy Book of Women's Mysteries
The Grandmother of Time
The Goddess in the Office
Grandmother Moon
The Goddess in the Bedroom
Summoning the Fates

INDEX

A

Alchemy, 34
Alexander, Skye, 159-165
Angus, 43
Anu, 43
Aplu, 104
Apprentice to Power, 136, 139
Artimite, 104
Astrology, 163-164

B

Bast, 44, 152
Bast-Wicca, tradition, 153

Beliefs, standing up for, 11-13
Black Forest Clan and
   Seminary, 112
Boann, 43
Book of Shadows, 80
Brittic tradition, 101
Buckland, Raymond, 117-124
Budapest, Z., 177-184
Buddha, 44

C

Camera, a thought-
   photography, 35
Candle blessing, 131-132

Candlelight Spells, 151
Ceres, 104
Charmed Life, A, 61
Circle Network, 56
College of the Sun, the, 38
Concept,
    oneness, 35
    Pagan, 35
    thought equals
        energy, 34-35
Cosmic consciousness, 159
Coven Mandragora, 152
Covenant of the Goddess, 132
Coventina, 43
Crystal
    charging, 131-132
    power of, 32-33
    skulls, 34
Currot, Phyllis, 79-95
Cyber Spellbook, The, 47

D

Dagda, 43
Dakin, Henry, 32
Dark Moon Mysteries, 136, 140
De La Warr Radionics
    Camera, 35
Demeter, 182
Diana, 172
Divine, 40-42
Dream Magic, 49

Drew, A.J., 69-77
Druidism, 35-37
    Gwyddonic, 35-37
Dunwich, Gerina, 147-157

E

Earth Magic, 168
Earth, Mother, 44, 106
EarthDance Collective,
    137-139
Edinborough Castle, 30
Enchantments of the Heart, 51
*Encyclopedia of Wicca and
    Witchcraft, The,* 97
Energies, male and female,
    40-42
Euro-Wicca, 111-112
Everyday Magic, 51
Exploring Celtic Druidism, 38
Exploring Wicca, 127

F

Female, honoring the, 40-42
Folk magick, 15
Freedom, 13-14
    religious, 13-14
Frey, 44
Freya, 44

G

Gardening With the Goddess, 61
Goddess In My Pocket, 61
Goddess in the Bedroom, 182
Goddess in the Office, 182
Grandmother Moon, 182
Grandmother of Time, 182
Gray, John, Dr., 41
Greenfire: Making Love with the Goddess, 37
Grimassi, Raven, 97-106
Gwydion, 43

H

Halloween!, 108
Handy Guide to the I Ching, 168
Harrison, Jane, 180
Healing, 90-91
Hectate, 130
Hedge Witchcraft, 122
Heimdall, 44
Holy Book of Women's Mysteries, 182

I

I Ching, 172
In Praise of the Crone, 51

International Pagan Conference, 47
Internet, 47
Intolerance, 15-16
Invisible castle, 173-174
Isis, 44, 152

K

Kali, 44
Kernunnos, 43, 131, 172
Kerridwen, 43, 131
Kirlian photography, 31-32
Kore, 182
Krippner, Stanley, 32
Krishna, 44

L

Lady Sabrina, 125-133
Lugh, 43

M

Magical Blend, 48
Magick,
    automatic, 74-75
    common definition of, 88-89
    folk, 15
    intention, 46-47
    natural, 74-75
    rapport, 46-47
    visualization, 46-47

Magickal Astrology, 163

Mainstream, becoming, 60, 93-94

Math, 43

Meditation, 131-132

Mind and Body, 144

Minoan Sisterhood, 85-86

Mishlove, Jeffrey, 32

Morrison, Dorothy, 51-60

Moss, Thelma, 32

Mother Earth, 106

N

New Millennium Council of Witches, 58

O

Odin, 44

Once Unknown Familiar, The, 137

Our Lady of Enchantment, 126-127

P

Paganism, Patriotic, 45-46

Pan, 172

Path, spiritual, 50

Patricia Telesco, 61-68

Philosophy, spiritual, 62

Photography, Kirlian, 31-32

Pictish-Gaelic tradition, 102

Positive Magic: Occult Self-Help, 167

Power,
sacred, earth, 44
sacred, elements, 44

Prayer chest, 131-132

Profiles in Courage, 12-13

Q

Questions, authors answered, 17-19

R

Raven's Call, 97-98

Raven's Loft, 98

Ravenwolf, Silver, 107-116

Real Witches Ball, 76-77

Rhiannon, 43

Roderick, Timothy, 135-145

Rosemerta, 43

S

Sabbat energy, 131

Sacred, the, 95

Salem West, 77

Search and rescue, 172-173

Seax-Wicca tradition, 120

Selene, 172

Shakti, 44

Shiva, 44
Skuld, 44, 180
Skulls, crystal, 34
Smithson, James, 30
Solitary practitioners, 120
Spirituality, fastest-growing, 14
Summoning the Fates, 182

T

Talisman, 131-132
Tarot cards, 29
Tart, Charles, 32
Thor, 44
Three Fates, The, 80
Threefold Law, 87-88
365 Goddesses, 61
To Ride a Silver Broomstick, 108
To Stir a Magic Cauldron, 108
Tradition,
    Bast-Wicca, 153
    Brittic, 101
    family, 42
    magickal, 62
    Pictish-Gaelic, 102
    Seax-Wicca, 120
    spiritual, 62
Transformational, magic as, 142-143

Triana, 43
Truth, divine, 14

U

Union, sacred, 45
Urd, 44, 180

V

Verdandi, 44, 180
Victorian Grimoire, A, 56
Vogel, Marcel, 32-35
Voodoo, 117

W

Weinstein, Marion, 167-175
What Witches Do, 129
Whimsical Tarot, The, 51
Wicca for Men, 69
Wicca Spellcraft for Men, 69
Wicca, English, 101
Wicca: A Guide for the Solitary Practitioner, 74
Wiccan Mysteries, The, 97
Wiccan Rede, 40
Wiccan Web, The, 47
Witch Crafting: A Spiritual Guide to Making Magic, 86
Witch's Beverages and Brews, A, 61

Witch's Master Grimoire, The, 127

Witchcraft Ancient and Modern, 121

Witchcraft, Basque, 101 Hedge, 122

Witchcraft...The Religion, 121 Witches, "Hollywood," 46 *Witches' Workbook, The*, 128

Y

Your Magickal Cat, 152

ABOUT THE AUTHOR

Sirona Knight lives in the Sierra Foothills of Northern California with her family: Michael, her husband of 26 years, and Skylor, their 10-year-old son, four beagles, and a family of cats. Sirona's ancestors include James Smithson, founder of the Smithsonian Institute, and she comes from a long line of the Daughters of the Revolution. She enjoys music, writing poetry, reading, surfing the Internet, as well as homeschooling her son, swimming, watching classic movies, and tending her garden.

Practicing magic for more than 17 years, Sirona is a Third Degree Craft Master of the Celtic Druid Tradition and the High Priestess of the College of the Sun in Northern California. She is the published author of several books on magick, and is the creator and author of the award-winning "Shapeshifter Tarot" deck. In addition, Sirona is a contributing editor for *Magical Blend* magazine. She makes media appearances, both radio and television, and maintains strong

Internet visibility through her Web site *(www.sironaknight.com)* and answering e-mail from readers and chatting on Web sites across the United States. Sirona's e-mail address is: bluesky@dcsi.net.

Other Books by Sirona Knight:

Exploring Celtic Druidism
The Witch and Wizard Training Guide
The Wiccan Spell Kit
Dream Magic
Celtic Traditions
The Little Giant Encyclopedia of Runes
Love, Sex, and Magick
The Shapeshifter Tarot
The Pocket Guide to Celtic Spirituality
The Pocket Guide to Crystals and Gemstones
Moonflower
Greenfire
The Wiccan Web (with Trish Telesco)

Forthcoming Books:

The Cyber Spellbook (with Trish Telesco)
Goddess Bless!
Practical Wicca
Faery Magick
Rune Magick